THEATRE GHOSTS

Her Majesty's Theatre designed by C. J. Phipps for Herbert Beerbohm Tree and opened in 1897

Roy Harley Lewis presents

THEATRE GHOSTS

Anthony Bate and the Bedevilled Piano

Leslie Crowther's Performing Butterfly

Evelyn Laye and the Grey Lady

Donald Sinden and the Vanishing Star

**The Vibrating Coat Hangers, featuring
Tony Britton and Sir Harry Secombe**

**The mysteries of the Hairy Legs, starring
Stanley Lupino and Margaret Rutherford**

★ ★ ★

*All-star bill supported by a unique
cast of celebrated ghosts and
outrageous poltergeists*

DAVID & CHARLES
Newton Abbot   London   North Pomfret (Vt)

The line drawings of Theatre Royal, Drury Lane are reproduced by courtesy of George Hoare, archivist; etchings of Her Majesty's Theatre, London, the Theatre Royal, Haymarket and interior of the Adelphi Theatre, by courtesy of the Theatre Museum, London; line drawings of the souvenir programme and Signor Pepi's box at the New Hippodrome Theatre, Darlington, by courtesy of the Civic, Darlington; Tameside Theatre ghost cartoon by courtesy of the Manchester Evening News; drawing of Eden Court Theatre, Inverness, by courtesy of the theatre; and the John Constable drawing of the Theatre Royal, Bath by courtesy of Barbara Litherland.

British Library Cataloguing in Publication Data

Lewis, Roy Harley
  Theatre ghosts.
  1. Theatres. Ghosts, to 1988
  I. Title
  133.1'22

ISBN 0-7153-9163-1

Typeset by Typesetters (Birmingham) Ltd
Smethwick, Warley, West Midlands
and printed in Great Britain by
Billing Limited, Worcester
for David & Charles (Publishers) plc
Brunel House   Newton Abbot   Devon

Published in the United States of America
by David & Charles Inc
North Pomfret   Vermont 05053   USA

CONTENTS

To Duncan and Jay,
for the idea

INTRODUCTION

Most people speculate about ghosts at one time or another; since we all have to die, the fascination with death is as natural as it is inevitable. And human nature being what it is, the more bizarre the circumstances of death, the more they grip the imagination. Yet in theatre, exclusively, it is the *setting* that captures and holds our attention, because theatre ghosts represent a slice of drama that is larger than life – and death.

Rife with superstition, the playhouse provides an environment in which we are encouraged to suspend reality; where every effort is made to attain the conducive air of 'magic' conjured up by the 'live' performance. Obviously, for much the same reason, a substantial number of rumoured sightings must be attributed to figments of such heightened imagination, or even wishful thinking. Yet, as you will discover, the majority of established 'resident' ghosts cannot be shrugged off lightly. If only a quarter of the reports were to survive the most thorough evaluation, they would provide more than enough evidence of a special relationship between theatre and the supernatural.

We live in an age when a mounting accumulation of knowledge provides the answers to so many of what were once apparently unfathomable riddles. Even in areas where speculation may not be replaced by fact for many years to come, at least this knowledge discourages us from rushing to judgement. Ghosts come into this 'pending' category; there are those who believe implicitly, accepting the flimsiest of information as gospel; those with equal conviction who scoff regardless – and the silent majority who wait to be convinced.

As family and friends on my mother's side were unquestioning spiritualists, my interest in the subject was predestined, although teenage enthusiasm was tempered by the failure of each and every one of my kinsfolk to make contact from beyond the grave. It could be argued that a somewhat jaundiced attitude was counter-productive; certainly in years of research I never had any supernatural experience that was totally convincing. On the other hand, there were strange incidents which defied explanation – enough to persuade me to continue reserving judgement.

'Ghosts' is a simple and conveniently vague broad heading. Most dictionaries settle for 'apparition', but that is only part of the story because hauntings are not necessarily accompanied by a visual presence – in the majority of cases, ghosts have been detected or recognised by the other senses. The French *revenant*, which means 'to come back' (from the dead), has an inference which seems nearer the mark, except for the presumption that the spirit ever left the haunted site to cross over into an afterlife.

So, what *is* a ghost? An apparition is to all intents and purposes the image of a dead person, 'stuck' in the transitionary stage that is said to exist after the earthly body has ceased to function – or, as the horrible new technocrat jargon would have it: there is 'negative patient output'! It is when there is no visible form that the question becomes more complex – unless it is simply that few people have the ability to *see* into another dimension. If we accept the premise that the human race, having evolved from a more primitive species, continues to develop, it is reasonable to suggest that in the not-too-distant future mankind will have powers that today are still difficult to comprehend. Meanwhile, ordinary people are aware of the three dimensions, and a limited few, usually clairvoyants, have the ability to recognise the fourth dimension – time – which would remove one of the apparent barriers between life and death.

Science has made all these concepts more acceptable. We know, for example, that in space flight a few years hence, the crew of a 'ship' travelling faster than the speed of light, would return from a journey to the stars considerably younger than the people left behind on Earth. But forgetting such romantic dreams – real enough though space travel will become – what would our great great-grandparents have made of live TV transmission? Scientists have long since identified and analysed light and sound to the extent that we can understand how radio waves or television pictures are transmitted and received. However, the study of other 'invisible' forms of energy – thought waves, for example, or less easily definable *impulses* given off by inanimate objects – is still in its infancy.

Over the years I have met investigators for the Society for Psychical Research, individuals who operated on the principle of not accepting anything on trust until it could be 'proved' to their satisfaction; in the main, a very down-to-earth group whose extensive experience enabled them to talk with authority. Yet in several instances, what impressed me most, was their gift of 'supersensory', or paranormal powers – something they accepted as normal as a talent for painting, or playing a musical instrument. One former colleague, a retired army officer, whose powers were so spectacular he could have made a living as an entertainer, would hold a personal object and 'convert' what he described as pulses of energy released from the object, into a stream of information relating to the owner. Unlike many professional mediums, who feed on unwitting clues – he would insist on silence, close his eyes, and start 'transmitting'.

The same man was able to demonstrate that buildings as well as objects, soak up atmosphere – retaining the essence of significant events in the manner of a time capsule, and that certain people are capable of picking up, or 'receiving' that stored information. The principle of photography provides a simple analogy – a ghostly spectre being the 'image' retained by an atmosphere or environment that may be as conducive as sensitised film stock. One has only to visit a very old building which has been the scene of a stream of dramatic events over centuries, to accept that the very stone seems to possess some of the qualities of recording tape or photographic negative in retaining *impressions* left by some of those events; impressions which may be of mood, or of stronger vibrations, clear enough to be identified by a person with the right gifts; even a force strong enough to evoke a 'physical' presence.

However, there is not necessarily any link between age or antiquity and the paranormal, and I began the research for this book aware that too many of the 'groans' and strange noises in old theatres, blithely attributed to dead souls in torment, were caused by a building cooling down after an audience has left, or the effects of suspended scenery and cloths moving in the draughts backstage – even the contractions of hemp rope from the grid. In fact, most 'ghostly' sounds have a rational explanation, coming even from antiquated central heating systems.

On the other hand, one does not necessarily have to be gifted in any way to *feel* the presence of a ghost. Most ordinary people are conscious of atmosphere; they can, for example, sense whether a house has a happy or depressed ambience. The key is to maintain a receptive frame of mind; to unshackle the imagination.

Theatre, we know, is larger than life – a place where imagination is nurtured and stretched, and where superstition abounds. This receptive atmosphere, coupled with that element of 'magic', opens a door to the past – to a storehouse of memories and the phasma of history, and to the spirit world. I have not attempted to differentiate between what might be regarded as a 'normal' ghost and the 'neurotic' poltergeist, because it is not important in the context of what is intended as a guide to haunted theatres. Nor have I attempted to explain certain apparent inconsistencies, such as why a spirit's footsteps should be heard when it has no material form, or why it should use doors to move from room to room, when it is apparently capable of simply passing through brick walls. The most logical theories have to do with time – what the ghost could see in his or her own time – but that is a complex issue dealt with more appropriately in other books. All I will say at the outset is that the incidents I have reported are, to the best of my knowledge, completely true – and offer evidence enough to impress even the most sceptical . . .

1

A Gathering Of
Ghosts – Drury Lane

Superstition would have us believe that a ghost in residence is lucky; that the spirit keeps a protective eye on things. Even more fortunate is the handful of privileged theatres which may have more than one – but any more would be stretching credibility, unless the evidence is too overwhelming to be challenged. However, there is one playhouse which is almost as famous for its convocation of ghosts as its succession of long-running musicals. Indeed, the perfect present for the rich spiritualist who has everything, would be a private visit to London's Theatre Royal, Drury Lane, where they could dispense with the formal seance and customary question: 'Is there anyone there?' – and simply instruct the spirits to wait in line!

Unquestionably the world's most haunted theatre, Drury Lane houses a whole family of ghosts from the unashamedly theatrical to the mundane – if it is not patronising to so describe former employees. In fact, there are several as yet unidentified, and my own researches uncovered at least one more of which management had no knowledge. In visual terms, their most eye-catching 'resident' is the Man in Grey, whose origins are not known, although it is somewhat fancifully assumed that he is the spectre of a man whose skeleton was discovered – a dagger plunged between the ribs – walled up in a secret chamber, almost 150 years ago. Although everything about him is speculation, the grisly remains were real enough, being buried in what is now a disused graveyard, a couple of hundred yards from the theatre, which can be seen from some upstairs windows – but despite an inquest there is no evidence to his identity; nor has subsequent detective work thrown any light on the mystery.

Theatre Royal, Drury Lane, 1812

The coroner actually recorded an open verdict, but we can surely assume the man did not stab himself, and as there has been a theatre on the site since 1661 it is reasonable to suppose that the murdered man was an actor, and the theory is supported by the Man in Grey's theatrical appearance. Indeed, the ghost presents a striking figure. Under a tricorn hat he wears a white wig, or perhaps his own hair fashionably powdered. The most distinguishing feature of his dress is a long grey cloak, worn over a white ruffle-fronted shirt, riding breeches and high boots; he is never without a dress sword.

The Man in Grey has been seen on many dozens of occasions since the 1930s, yet not before – which I find surprising as he would have been killed over a century earlier. This, together with the circumstances of his 'discovery' disturbs me a little, and is why I find Drury Lane's other ghosts of greater interest. The story is such a 'natural' to anyone even remotely romantic, that his existence is usually accepted without hesitation. For example, George Hoare, a former general manager and theatre archivist since his retirement, conducts tours of the building for various parties, including the new casts of long-running shows. 'I've got into the habit of pointing out where the Man in Grey has been seen', he says. 'Within a week or so practically everyone in the cast is convinced that they have also seen him, and schoolchildren see him in every shadow.'

The first indication of his presence was heralded with more than a degree of showmanship by theatre historian and writer, W. J. Macqueen Pope shortly before World War II when his own sightings had been confirmed by a cleaner who saw what she thought was an actor sitting in the upper circle, watching a rehearsal on stage. When she approached to pass the time of day, the figure rose and moved off – finally disappearing *through* the wall. While 'Popie' was a respected historian, and I have no doubt that he actually saw the Man in Grey on several occasions, before and after the war, those close to him concede that he was also a great showman, and it was undoubtedly through his well publicised sightings that the Man in Grey became an 'overnight' celebrity.

To illustrate the point, it was 'Popie' who came up with the most romantic theory of the ghost's identity. While other witnesses – and they include not only many individuals, but on one occasion in 1939 more than half the cast of *The Dancing Years* assembled on stage for a photocall, who saw him cross the upper circle – have gained only a general impression, with minor variances of dress (eg sometimes the hat is worn, sometimes he is bareheaded), Macqueen Pope is the only person on record who was able to describe the Man in Grey as 'young', and 'handsome'. On the basis of that 'evidence', it may have seemed reasonable for him to suggest that at some time in the eighteenth century, a young actor fell in love with a pretty girl under the 'protection' of the theatre manager; that the rivals quarrelled over her and the younger man was stabbed to death; his body concealed in a hastily erected bricked-up chamber. However, that was pure conjecture; all we know for certain is that during structural alterations 150 years ago, workmen in the upper circle reported that part of the main wall sounded hollow. Since that conflicted with what was shown on the plans, the wall was knocked down – and the skeleton discovered. It had been there for many years, because the remains of clothing covering the bones soon crumbled to dust.

It is through the repaired wall that the Man in Grey starts or finishes his leisurely stroll, although there have been several sightings of him in other parts of the theatre. The only other certainty is that he never appears at night, or in the hours of darkness; indeed, Macqueen Pope established to his own satisfaction that he only appeared between the hours of 9am and 6pm, although never to order – especially when summoned by interested parties from outside, such as the psychic investigators and BBC radio researchers who have been drawn to Drury Lane.

George Hoare, general manager from 1958 until he took 'early' retirement at the age of seventy-one in 1982, has never seen the Man in Grey, or any of the resident ghosts, although he has had some very strange experiences. A very down-to-earth person, Mr Hoare endeavours to assess each reported incident on its apparent merits, but while he remains sceptical of many reports (there were, incidentally, some suggestions that Macqueen Pope's almost regular sightings could have been due to thought-projection), has no doubt that the building is haunted by a number of different ghosts, some of them not as 'passive' as the Man in Grey. He also believes that 'happenings', as opposed to mere sightings come in cycles; one show might be beset with inexplicable incidents, the next might be trouble free – although in all cases the incidents are of a joking or mischievous nature, never malicious. The Drury Lane 'resident' ghosts are nothing but good natured spirits.

George Hoare's file on the subject includes a letter from a clairvoyant who wrote from the North of England to claim that he had been in touch on the spirit plane with the Man in Grey, who had identified himself as Arnold Woodruffe, and that if confronted with the words: 'What ails thee, friend Arnold', he would finally go to his rest. But the name Woodruffe does not appear anywhere in the theatre's well-documented history, although the manager of Edmund Kean was a Samuel Arnold. In any case, the whole issue of 'troubled' spirits unable to find their way into the afterlife, is somewhat confusing because so many theatre ghosts are former actors or managers who remain *because* they loved the place so much. Indeed, George Hoare believes when the time comes, he may well stay on himself to join the spirits assembled at Drury Lane.

Another experience of mediums in action was more impressive. Having had a psychic experience some years earlier when

14

attending a performance of *Chorus Line* (described later), clairvoyant Wendy Francis visited Drury Lane by invitation on the morning of 23 April 1983; she was accompanied by a woman friend, who was not a spiritualist. Although she had heard of the Man in Grey, she knew little of the theatre's history, still less of the people who had worked there, which makes her report – handwritten at the time, without the opportunity to elaborate, or polish the somewhat disjointed style – so fascinating. I shall include excerpts, but as we are concerned for the moment with the Man in Grey, this is what she recalled of her visit to the upper circle in the company of Mr Hoare, and her friend. In fact, she encountered the ghost only after meeting an apparition which George later identified from her detailed description, as a former house-keeper at the theatre.

Dealing with the Man in Grey – or 'Arnold', as she knew him from his publicity – she wrote '. . . It is easy to claim it was auto-suggestion, but there were three of us there, all with varying beliefs and ideas. [NB: During the entire three-hour session, George Hoare did not see anything untoward, but remained convinced of the medium's integrity] . . . It did not take long for Arnold's curiosity to be aroused, and put in an appearance to find out what we were about. As we continued to stand in the gallery I noticed him making his way towards us to our right. He walked about ten paces, stopped for a while, walked a few more paces, stopped and stood looking down at the stage – and after a few seconds slowly began walking towards us again. I made up my mind to say nothing to the others; I wanted to see if they too felt or saw anything. When Arnold was just a few feet from us, my friend said a little nervously: "He's here, isn't he?" I told her to take no notice, that he was just curious.

'Arnold stood behind us. He made us all very aware of his presence by this time [NB: George Hoare cannot recall the incident in detail, but although he had never seen any apparition he has many times been conscious of an icy-cold "presence" that was distinctly unearthly]. He seemed curious yet benign – a strange little man, full of mischief, yet at the same time solemn. How to describe him? He appeared not very tall, about 5ft 6 inches – 5ft 7 inches, dressed rather untidily in a button down smock/shirt, breeches, brown boots almost knee length. His hair – I thought a wig – shoulder length, grey, resembling untidy ringlets. He had a thin moustache, and was wearing little "metal" rimmed spectacles. I feel his appearance was rather deceptive, because although fairly untidy in dress (he was carrying a hat and wearing no jacket) I think in his day he carried some weight; a very clever, knowledgeable man, especially with money, full of insight, although somewhat eccentric. I would put him around 1820 onward. I feel a connection with Kean. His dress strikes me as odd, almost as though borrowed from wardrobe. Arnold is full of concern for the theatre's welfare and those connected with it; I don't think I would like to encounter Arnold if I intended any harm. As it was, we all began to feel at ease with him.' According to Wendy Francis, 'Arnold' accompanied them for the rest of the tour, during which she encountered other identifiable phenomena.

Apart from the fact that in the royal box he tugged 'playfully' at her hair, which would be the first report that he had 'interfered' with anyone, the most impressive feature – at least, to me – of her account is the difference between this description and the more romanticised version of Macqueen Pope, which is the only account which could have influenced her in advance. It would also knock on the head the story of the handsome young actor murdered by a villainous manager; if she is to be believed, then it is more likely to have been the older man who was murdered!

The only other unusual picture of the Man in Grey (in all the other sightings, he did not show any interest in people) was during a performance of *Carousel* in 1950 when one of the stars, Morgan Davies on stage, looked up to see what appeared to be the only empty seat in the house – in a box. But when he looked again he noticed a figure in a long grey cloak open at the front to a shirt with long sleeves and ruffled cuffs. After sitting quietly for several minutes the man then stood up and lifted an arm – which was transparent!

I referred earlier to buildings which become storehouses of memories, and Wendy Francis's initial impression of Drury Lane when trying to concentrate on the performance of *Chorus Line* was of the 'incredible atmosphere' ('. . . never during my course of work have I been inside a building so full of every kind of emotion, love, loyalty and inspiration'), and this is hardly surprising since there have been four theatres on the site, each with its own fascinating story.

Samuel Pepys watched the construction of the first theatre on the site, already a regular visitor to the other royal venue, the Duke's Playhouse, opened two years earlier in Lincoln's Inn Fields. Playgoing in the seventeenth century had its hazards, as Pepys' diary entry for 2 July 1661 indicates: '. . . To Sir William Davenant's Opera; this being the fourth day that it hath begun, and the first time that I have seen it . . . And by the breaking of a board over our heads, we had a great deal of dust fell into the ladies' necks and the men's hair, which made great sport . . .'

The Duke's Playhouse did not survive, although it was still there in January 1672 when the Theatre Royal company moved following the destruction by fire of their first home. Pepys had missed the opening performance at Drury Lane, but his diary for 8 May 1663 reveals: '. . . Thence to my brother's, and there took my wife and Ashwell [her maid] to the Theatre Royall, being the second day of its being opened . . . [NB the production was Beaumont and Fletcher's *The Humorous Lieutenant*, which did not much appeal to him.] The house is made with extraordinary good contrivance, and yet hath some faults, as the . . .' Pepys was a shrewd judge, and there were to be design changes.

Of all the ghosts associated with Drury Lane, there has never been any sign of Pepys' favourites, Mrs Knipp, who had talent as well as a pretty face, or Nell Gwynne, the King's mistress who was given the opportunity to act after selling oranges in the Pit. Ironically, for all her claims to be a 'legitimate' actress (she made her debut in 1665 in Dryden's *The Indian Emperor*) poor Nell's ghost did not make the Theatre Royal, ending up instead at the Gargoyle strip club in Soho. How she came to be identified there is not known – the only clue being the scent of gardenias – so if the club really is haunted, the ghost is probably an impostor!

The second playhouse on the site, which was built by Sir Christopher Wren in 1674 and demolished in 1791, is best remembered for the famous actors and plays associated

17

with it, names such as Charles Kemble, Sarah Siddons, David Garrick – also the manager for many years, to be succeeded by Richard Brinsley Sheridan, whose *The School for Scandal* was first performed here in 1775. One of the reported ghosts from this period is that of Charles Macklin who killed a fellow actor in the theatre's Green Room. It was the force of Macklin's personality, and his enduring stamina as an actor (still working at ninety, when he starred as Shylock in *The Merchant of Venice*, he lived until over a hundred) that may have enabled his spirit to survive the centuries, rather than the man he killed, Thomas Hallam. A very tall, thin, hot-tempered Irishman, Macklin had a reputation for quarrelling, and during one outburst in 1735 he lunged at Hallam with his stick, which pierced the actor's eye, causing his death. Macklin's ghost, identified from contemporary drawings, has been seen on a number of occasions, usually in the early evening when the fight took place.

The third building, commissioned by Sheridan and built in 1794 was destroyed by fire in 1809, and the present one dates from three years later, making it the oldest playhouse in London. In each case Drury Lane continued to make news off-stage as well as on. In 1800, George III, sitting in the royal box, survived an assassination attempt, and not long after the opening of the present building, the same monarch caused a scandal by publicly 'boxing' the ears of his son, the Prince Regent. Because of their unconcealed enmity and to prevent a reoccurrence of the scene, signs were installed reading 'King's Side' and 'Prince's Side' over the approaches to facing boxes.

The ghosts of two outstanding artistes associated with the present building – Edmund Kean and Dan Leno, of different periods and vastly different styles – have also been identified at different times. Rumours abound and become distorted in re-telling, and unfortunately I have been unable to trace anyone who actually saw the former. However, the medium Wendy Francis, during her tour of the theatre, stood for a while in the royal box, and while looking down at the stage reported seeing a man in period costume parading up and down in a dramatic manner. Having no idea who he might have been, she gave George Hoare a full description, which at that moment did not mean much to him either. She conceded in her report that, in the knowledge of hundreds of actors having been on that stage, auto-suggestion could not be ruled out, but insisting that she had never seen pictures of any of them, especially in costume – yet Mr Hoare was later able to pull out a print of Edmund Kean, matching her description in almost every respect. However, auto-suggestion *is* too great a possibility to place much credence on that incident.

Macqueen Pope had an intriguing story about the ghost of Kean's actor son, Charles Kean, in whose arms he died on stage after a production of *Othello*. The author received a letter from sisters who had attended a matinee performance in the company of their brother. Before the curtain went up, the ladies were fascinated by the appearance of a man only a few feet away from them in the same row of the dress circle. Although his hair was exceptionally long, what surprised them most, was his style of dress, which might have been fashionable a hundred years before. Taken aback, they discreetly drew the man's unusual appearance to the attention of their brother – but his only reaction was surprise that they could see anyone at all; as far as he was concerned, the seat was unoccupied. Their attention was focussed elsewhere as the lights went down for the start of the play. At the end of the first act they instinctively looked back at the stranger, but he had disappeared – which amazed them because he could not have left without disturbing them at the end of the row. The identity of the strange figure remained a mystery until one of the sisters subsequently read Macqueen Pope's book on the history of the Theatre Royal, and promptly recognised the lesser known of the two Keans.

Dan Leno (1860–1904) began his show business career at the age of four, appearing with his older brother and uncle, as a dancer. At eighteen he was a champion clog dancer – and his versatility is one reason why he was a success in pantomime. However, it was as a comedian he became famous, and at the peak of his career in 1901, after a royal command performance, he was known as the King's Jester, and even had a children's comic named after him. Unfortunately, overwork led to a nervous breakdown which culminated in insanity,

19

although his ghost seems to have the same benign aura as the others. In his fascinating autobiography, *From Stocks to the Stars* (Hutchinson 1934), Stanley Lupino, the popular comedian-dancer (1893–1942), of the multi-talented Lupino family, related a couple of experiences which happened to him in Leno's dressing room.

The first was during a pantomime season when, one night after it had snowed heavily, he set off for home but found the icy roads so bad he was constantly skidding; finally running into an advertising hoarding and damaging the car's front axle. Lupino went back to the theatre to sleep in his dressing room, borrowing a stage bed and bedclothes from the props store. There was no central heating in those days, so after building up the fire, he switched off the light and got into bed. The author made a point of stating that he was 'stone-cold' sober; also that the dressing room was small, with a section curtained off for his clothes. There was only one door, which he had instinctively locked. He was lying in total silence when, after a few minutes, he heard the sound of the curtain being drawn. Since there was no one else in the room he sat up in alarm. In the eerie glow of the fire, he saw a pair of legs – as though a man was standing with his back to the fire, and looking across and down at him.

'Only the legs were visible,' the account continues: 'I was about to spring off the bed when the legs began to move away. I watched as they disappeared into the shadows. The door opened and clanged back – the iron door I had bolted! I sprang up. My first action was to switch on the light. I looked round me. I *had* heard the curtains drawn aside – they were still drawn back. Then to the door. That was shut. It was still bolted on the inside.'

Elsewhere in the chapter he writes: 'This time my visitor came when all the lights were on, and the noise could be heard from the street of the people outside my window waiting to be let into the theatre. I was making up and quite unprepared for what happened. As I was looking in the glass, I suddenly saw another face appear above mine. It was looking at me with a smile, and was also in make-up. There was a line across the forehead where a wig had been removed.

'There was no mistaking that face. I had seen it many

times in photographs and paintings. There was no doubt in my mind as I gazed at the reflection that I was looking into the face of Dan Leno!

'Naturally I thought it was someone having a big joke at my expense. I winked. The face winked back. Then I swung round. The room was empty.

'I was alert for any sound. There was the noise from the street, but in the room it was perfectly quiet. The door was shut. I next surmised that it had been a reflection caused, if not by a trickster, then by some accident of the light or movement of the mirror. I placed the glass at all angles and tried all kinds of experiment, but to no avail. Later I learned that the room had been a favourite one of Dan Leno, and the last one he had dressed in for the stage.'

There was an interesting sequel. Two nights later, Lupino was sitting in the room, accompanied by his wife and one of her friends. When he was called to go on stage, and left the room he heard his wife's friend gasp with what seemed like surprise. He turned to see his wife react, and ask what the matter was. 'That man gave me such a turn,' the friend replied.

'What man?' demanded Mrs Lupino.

'That little fellow who was behind the curtain and followed Stanley out!'

Stanley Lupino was not a spiritualist, but maintained that he kept an open mind on the subject, and those who knew him well insist that they believe every word of his anecdotes. It was not a subject he would have lied about.

There are other less convincing reports of Leno's unearthly face materialising in the same dressing room mirror, including one from a girl dancer who set out to spend the night in the room – and then got the fright of her life, cutting the plan short; other tales of sounds resembling the type of noises Dan Leno might have made in practising his dance routines before a show. However, as I suggested earlier, 'noises' are the most common feature of theatre phenomena and more often than not have an ordinary explanation. Auto-suggestion is another problem. During a period when evidence pointed to genuine supernatural goings-on at London's Garrick Theatre, several people insisted that the ghost's presence was signalled by an unpleasant smell.

Further investigation, however, revealed a fault in the drains!

The ghosts identified so far have all been relatively passive, but there are undoubtedly a number of spirits who take a more active interest in what is going on, many to offer a helping hand which might be considered of benefit to the production, but occasionally mischievous. There is little clue as to which ghost this might be. Is it one and the same spirit, for example, who has come to the assistance of various artistes on stage, particularly in the musicals for which Drury Lane is best known? Macqueen Pope, who knew more about the theatre than anyone, told the story of one of the American stars of *Oklahoma*, Betty Jo Jones who, unfamiliar with the huge stage, felt herself physically guided by the hands of an unseen stage director into a much better position (remember, every show is carefully 'blocked' in rehearsal, which means that performers should know instinctively where they should be at any moment) and next time, knowing her invisible helper had been correct, she moved to the new place of her own accord – to be rewarded by an approving pat on the back! Something similar happened during auditions for *The King and I*, when the actress Doreen Duke was convinced of two supportive hands guiding her, followed by a pat on the back.

However, despite the remarkably happy ambience at Drury Lane, there are many other more disconcerting stories. The belief that old theatres have an atmosphere of their own is taken a stage further by people in the business, such as Robert Stanton who concluded a distinguished career in stage management by becoming head of the stage management faculty of the London Academy of Music & Dramatic Art, until his retirement in 1987. Stage manager at Drury Lane during the six-year run of My *Fair Lady*, Bob Stanton is convinced not only of a special aura, but even a distinct personality of its own (a view supported by George Hoare). 'It is as though the theatre is a living entity,' he says. 'Initially I had a sense of not being accepted – of being on trial, but gradually I was able to relax and found it as wonderful a place as I'd been told.'

In the years he worked at Drury Lane (and he had been there before, rehearsing other shows) he never saw a ghost, but he did have some strange experiences. On the opening night of

My *Fair Lady*, the sheer scale of the production necessitated his doing a variety of jobs in addition to co-ordinating the stage management team. For much of the evening he worked the prompt corner, alternating with his deputy, Harry Bowers. Immediately in front of him was a mini-set on wheels – 'stone' steps leading up to the front door of a house – which would be trucked on stage when required. Like all sets for major productions, it looked very realistic, but the flat surface at the top of the steps was covered with wooden boards.

Picture then the build-up to one of the hit numbers, 'The Rain In Spain', during which the stage area had to be kept hushed as Eliza Doolittle (Julie Andrews), struggled painfully with the relationship between rain, Spain, main(ly), and plain – indeed, 50/60 people usefully occupied backstage, had been moved off. In the relative silence, Bob Stanton, in the prompt corner, was suddenly aware of a creaking noise immediately in front of him, as though someone was moving on the top step of the stairs. Since he could see there was no one there, he looked up into the flies to see if someone was manipulating the flat (representing the front of the house), causing it to vibrate – but there was no one directly above. Nothing was moving, yet the creaking noise continued. Then the music started, and his attention was distracted.

He was too busy to think any more about the noise, but in the second act while Stanley Holloway was singing 'Get Me To The Church', Bob was in the same position, facing the stage and waiting to give the next cue when a hand was suddenly thrust into his left hand trousers' pocket. Startled by what he assumed was Harry Bowers 'skylarking', and in exasperation at such unprofessional behaviour on opening night, he instinctively swung the microphone in his right hand to strike the offending hand. The result was a bruised thigh, because not only was there no hand to cushion the blow, but there was nobody behind him. Of one thing he remains clear to this day – from the force with which it happened, and his own lightning reflexes, no person could have jumped out of the darkness and back again without being caught in the act.

At the end of the show, comparing notes, he reported both incidents, beginning to wonder if his imagination had been playing up – but Harry Bowers went 'white as a sheet'.

'I wasn't going to say anything,' Harry retorted, 'but when *I* was in the prompt corner, I heard the creaking sounds and in the first act someone clapped me on the shoulder – hard. I turned round quickly, but there was no one there!' Nevertheless, they treated the incidents as something of a joke, until they were overheard by Betty Woolf, the actress playing Professor Higgins' housekeeper, Mrs Pierce, whose re-action was 'Thank goodness it wasn't just *me!*' She had been just about to make her entrance via the same mini-set in the final scene of Act One when, standing alone, and nobody in sight, someone pinched her bottom!

The mysterious sounds on the step outside the front-door 'set' continued for the rest of the week, but there was no recurrence of any pranks throughout the rest of the run.

While it is impossible to identify unseen spirits, it is reason-able to speculate that a series of mischievous pranks might well be the work of one individual, eg jacket tugging seems to be a characteristic of one regular culprit. One incident actually happened on stage at the end of a performance of *No No Nanette* (1973), starring Anna Neagle and Tony Britton. For their cur-tain call the principals came to the front of the stage while a large chorus spread across the stage five to six feet behind them. When Tony Britton bowed he felt the right hand 'tail' of his evening suit tugged sharply, almost enough to throw him off balance. Involuntarily, he turned round, imagining the unimaginable – that one of the dancers was playing the fool – but as common sense indicated, everyone was intent on taking their own bows; in any case, they were too far behind to reach him. As Mr Britton had not heard of the mysteri-ous jacket-puller, the incident was shrugged off. However, one night during one of the big production numbers, he was waiting in the wings, enjoying the dancing while waiting his cue to go on. Then, as the dancers trooped off, breathing heavily and covered in perspiration, one of the girls leaned exhaustedly against a piece of scenery; she stood for a while, head bowed, waiting for her breathing to return to normal. Tony Britton was talking quietly to a member of the stage management team, some ten to fifteen feet away when they heard a shriek. They looked up and saw her whirl round with an indignant exclamation: 'Who did that?' When they asked her what the matter was, she complained that somebody had 'goosed' her! Yet it was a physical impossibility for any person to get close enough, unseen, to even lay a finger on her.

However, it was not until a third incident that Tony Britton began to wonder about other possibilities. He was in his dressing room, changing between scenes, and talking to a friend. Edward, his dresser, took a jacket from a metal hanger on the door, and when he put the empty hanger back the simple action caused it to vibrate very slightly, as might be expected. But instead of coming to rest, the vibration gathered momentum to such an extent that the conversation stopped and they became transfixed by the continual rattling. Then gradually it slowed to a halt. We know what happens when we place a light metal hanger back in its place; it may not stop dead. But this was anything but normal – it was a vibration that was sustained for about a minute.

Coincidentally, something very similar happened to Sir Harry Secombe, six years earlier, when he was starring in *The Four Musketeers*, the musical adaptation of the Dumas story. Sir Harry was sitting, alone, in his dressing room late at night when one of the metal coat hangers suddenly came to life. Twenty years later he clearly remembers the incident when the hanger went 'all peculiar', accompanied by a clear tapping on the wall – although he knew there was nobody about. This was the only strange experience, 'other than with audiences!', in a long career in show business, so he has had plenty of time to consider the possibilities – but he still has no explanation for the hanger which lost its cool.

The wardrobe department at Drury Lane is at the very top of a large rambling building, up several flights of stairs and long corridors. One night, towards the end of *No No Nanette*, the wardrobe mistress and her assistant were waiting for the costumes to be brought up for cleaning and any small repairs that might be needed. The door had been left open and they were able to hear the finale over the tannoy, so that when they heard footsteps approaching in the passage they assumed it was Tony Britton's dresser, Edward, because he was the youngest, fittest and always the first up. But as the footsteps became clearer, no one appeared in the open doorway – instead, an old plastic 'No Smoking' sign was hurled into

25

the centre of the room. Although alarmed, they impulsively rushed to the doorway, but there was no one there despite the sound of disappearing footsteps. If the footsteps had anything to do with the incident, there was no time for anyone to have got away.

The sequence prompted Tony Britton, with George Hoare's permission, to invite a medium to the theatre. The man he remembers as 'Tom' agreed to investigate if he was given a free hand to wander anywhere, and this was agreed. The clairvoyant had no connection with the theatre, and was given no time to research its history, yet without any fuss he 'saw' several of the resident ghosts, including the Man in Grey. But his most interesting report came during a major dance routine when principal dancer Teddy Green, supported by the chorus, was performing one of the show's most joyous production numbers. 'Tom' came over to Tony Britton and George Hoare, pointed to the centre of the swirling figures,

Theatre Royal today

and said he could see a little man 'with big boots', dancing with them, smiling broadly and having a great time. He went on to describe what was unseen to them, and when George Hoare subsequently produced a photograph to match the description, it was of Dan Leno, who had started his career as a clog dancer. It is, of course, possible that the medium had known about Dan Leno and was telling them what they would want to hear – but they believed he was genuine.

Despite this abundance of supernatural activity, not everyone has been able to see anything out of the ordinary, although there is an uncorroborated story of a sound technician who had been working in one of the top boxes, later going down via one of the corridors at the back of the upper circle (Man in Grey territory), when he saw a pair of feet walking towards him – with nothing above! But George Hoare has had too many strange experiences to doubt that his inability to 'see' what others have reported, is anything more than a lack of psychic perception.

Furthermore, he has seen the effect of sightings, not only on 'impressionable' theatre folk but on pet animals, such as the theatre cat, James, in the 1970s, and dogs brought in by special visitors – none of which would go into certain parts of the building, obviously petrified by something they could not understand. He has also experienced the sensation of sudden cold, particularly in the upper circle, which is supposed to denote the presence of 'something' not of this world, and – in physical terms – felt the presence of something else unseen.

Anyone who knows George Hoare will accept the premise that he is anything but gullible. But his personal experiences are not easily explained. As general manager he was expected to wear a dinner jacket during performances. On one occasion he went to his dressing room to change back into ordinary clothes and, stooping to reach the door handle, he was suddenly grabbed by the bottom of the jacket and pulled back sharply. He was alone at the time in a narrow, deserted corridor, and he had not been drinking! 'It was not something I could have imagined,' he told me. 'The tug was powerful enough to pull me off balance, yet there was no room for anyone to stand behind me.'

Rather more eerie was an experience repeated on a number

27

of occasions when he worked particularly late in his office. 'At times, especially during the long run of My *Fair Lady*, I might be in my office until after midnight,' he recalls. 'Suddenly the stillness would be shattered as the loose objects on my desk seemed to come to life. Pens and pencils, paper, sharpeners, and even odd coins, began to jump up and down – it seemed, angrily. It unnerved me considerably, yet when I took it as a hint and got up to leave, they settled down again.'

Something very similar happened late at night when he was elsewhere in the building, and his wife was waiting for him in the same office. It was too much for her and she fled. Since nothing more violent ever took place, George came to the conclusion that the disturbances were caused by the spirit of Arthur Collins, a general manager and director of the theatre between 1897–1923, because there is evidence that Collins would be annoyed with members of his staff who worked late, satisfied in his mind that an efficient person could complete his work within prescribed hours of business.

But presumably Collins was not consistently ill-humoured, because he has also turned up – and been seen – in less alarming circumstances. On one occasion during the run of My *Fair Lady*, two members of the cast – Freda Sessions, from the chorus, and Toni Lee, who took over from Julie Andrews as Eliza Doolittle – came to see the show during a week off. It may not occur to the average theatregoer, but performers never have the opportunity to see their own show from the front. The women were sitting in George Hoare's office when a man they had never seen before walked in, and ignoring them, crossed the room to open a cupboard. After a perfunctory inspection, he left. His silence and the strangeness of his manner scared them, although they had no reason to suppose it was a ghost, and when they subsequently described his appearance, George realised it was the Arthur Collins he had only seen in photographs.

Mr Hoare was impressed by what the medium, Wendy Francis, claimed to have seen, believing that even if her report written in his office was in some part the product of an active imagination, she had seen the spirits of people she could not possibly have known about, eg a former housekeeper whose existence had not been documented, except in name only.

On her previous visit six years earlier in the audience at a performance of *Chorus Line*, she had been distracted by the ambience of the place, different from that of any theatre she had visited. At one point her wandering attention became focussed on a box to her right in which sat a distinguished, elderly man. 'Although seated,' she recalled, 'I could tell he was fairly tall, slimmish, grey hair swept back, short neat sideburns, and he was wearing a monocle. I guessed his evening clothes were from around the 1930s, but one thing was certain – he was not part of that living audience.'

It was not until her meeting with George Hoare years later that her description prompted him to search through old photographs and come up with one of George Grossmith, a former managing director, matching her eye-witness account down to the last detail, including his mannerism of placing his hands together in a distinctive manner.

In the upper circle, before encountering 'Arnold', or the Man in Grey, she had stopped in mid-conversation at the sudden appearance of an elderly woman, who remained unseen by her companions. The apparition was wearing a scarf around her head, a 'scruffy' green jumper, calf-length dark brown skirt, old-fashioned lace-up shoes, and what appeared to be men's socks. 'She also wore glasses, and I got the impression that these were not really hers, but possibly borrowed; they were perched, almost on the end of her nose, and she was looking over the top.' Wendy reported. 'Although fairly frail, she had a definite air of authority – hands on hips as if questioning our presence.' The description tallied with George Hoare's memories of a Mrs Jordan who had been at Drury Lane for forty years, most of which in charge of the large cleaning staff.

I have always been a shade sceptical about some of the reports relating to the much publicised Man in Grey, although as there have been hundreds, a fair proportion may well have been genuine – that is, were not imagined. However, I fail to see any reason for a spiritualist to conjure up a rather 'ordinary' employee, not long 'passed over', about whom she could not have known. Even the commonly held theory that a clever medium can pick up clues from random thought memories does not stand up here. George Hoare was certainly not thinking about the old lady at the time; indeed his only vivid recollection of her was not in the building, but outside, supervising the dozen or so cleaners working in unison at the daily cleaning of the steps and massive foyer.

When Ray Mancell, manager at Her Majesty's, was at Drury Lane, he was watching the opening of a 1986 revival of *42nd Street* from outside the auditorium through the curtains covering the glass panelled doors. At his side were two usherettes. There was no one behind them so when he felt a tap on the shoulder he suspected one of his companions was forgetting her position and playing a joke. But when he saw how engrossed they were in the show he realised it could not have been either of the women. Shortly afterwards, one of them went into the auditorium, and instinctively he moved back slightly so that the remaining usherette remained in sight. Again he felt a tug at his jacket, and spun round expecting to find someone he knew – but there was no one. This time he found the usherette studying him, obviously wondering about his strange behaviour. 'I never saw anything during my spell there,' he concedes, 'but there were a number of strange incidents that defy explanation.'

Until the early 1970s Drury Lane employed two 'royal waiters', dressed in full eighteenth-century livery (white powdered wig, red coat, blue velvet breeches and pink stockings), to attend the three boxes on the King's Entrance side, and three on the Prince's side. They were very much part of the Theatre Royal tradition, which ended only when one of them died and could not be satisfactorily replaced. In 1957, Mildred Wood was singing in the chorus of different opera companies, and between engagements did temporary work – at one stage working in the general manager's office.

One winter afternoon about 5pm Mildred was returning from a brief visit to the dress circle, along the outside of the long bar when she came face to face with one of the royal waiters coming from the opposite direction. He smiled politely, inclining his head with period courtesy and she reciprocated spontaneously. She thought nothing more of the episode until a few days later when she asked George Hoare's secretary the identity of the man she had seen, describing him in detail. The secretary, Susan Cook, seemed puzzled by the

30

there. Yet as soon as I closed it again, the footsteps started – going back across the stage.'

On two occasions when he was involved in cinema duties the ghost or ghosts were in more mischievous mood. The first time he was sitting on top of the screen after it had been given a re-spray, and the screen began to shake so violently that he almost fell off. Assuming it was caused by the painters below he called down in protest and clung on, but when it continued to shake he managed to climb down, intending to give them a piece of his mind – but they had left the building some time before. On the other occasion he was in the projection box, running the film, and intent on watching the cue marks on the film ready to change reels. His concentration was suddenly disturbed by a tap on the shoulder, and he assumed that it was the projectionist from another cinema with whom he was friendly, and who would often pop in for a chat. 'Give over, Philip,' he exclaimed, and when the tap was repeated, his complaint held more than a note of exasperation. He turned round automatically – but there was nobody there.

Another sighting occurred late one night when he glanced through the glass panels at the sides of the circle foyer doors. There were small posters stuck over the glass so he could only see parts of the person outside, but it was reasonable to suppose it was the 'beat' policeman who often came in at about that time. He called out loudly, 'I'm in here,' but the figure did not respond and began to move away, so he followed him out, catching the back of him going downstairs. The figure still seemed unaware of him and continued down to the downstairs foyer which was pitch black. Jack followed keeping it in sight until it suddenly vanished in the darkness. Having confirmed that all the doors were locked, he knew there was no way a person could have got out of the theatre. By now he was convinced that the intruder was a burglar, but at that moment the policeman did arrive and together they searched the premises from top to bottom. 'Every door was locked so it was impossible for anyone to get in or out,' he maintains.

During the pantomime season in January 1977, the two stars – comedian Jack Douglas, and ventriloquist Keith Harris – were walking across the front of the stalls engaged in conversation when they became conscious of someone beckoning them from the back. It was difficult in the poor light to make out exactly who the person was but they somehow assumed it was Fred, the stage door keeper. They acknowledged that they had seen him and were coming in due course and carried on talking. However, when they saw him beckoning again they headed in his direction, although on arriving at the back of the stalls they realised the man they had kept in vision had either vanished into thin air – or they had walked through him. Jack Clark, near at hand, remembers the incident vividly because Jack Douglas was 'as white as a sheet', although Keith Harris seemed to take it in his stride. Ten years later Keith recalls a shadow-like figure, and admits he was not quite so cool, but that it did not register at first, and the initial reaction was followed by a sense of disbelief.

With dramatic cutbacks in mining and steel industries, South Wales might be regarded as one of Britain's depressed areas. But the city of Swansea supported by timely grants from the EEC was determined not only to survive, but to become a cultural centre for Wales and the West. Symbolic of this ambition was a £7$\frac{1}{2}$ million transformation of its famous Grand Theatre into what could ultimately be one of the most impressive arts complexes in Europe. The concept was to blend past and future by building above and around the existing theatre – preserving the original auditorium which has so much charm and character. The first phase, a huge pre-dominantly glass structure, incorporating an enlarged stage area and new fly tower with the latest electronic backstage equipment, was completed a few years ago, although further work continued until 1987.

The Grand offers a six-month repertory season plus panto-mime; the rest of the year being open to touring shows – and one of the incentives for embarking on the hugely am-bitious project was to offer better facilities to the larger companies on tour. The days are now gone when shoppers were transfixed by the sight of traffic being held up by members of the visiting Welsh National Opera carrying scenery across the road from a make-shift store in the bus station!

The story of the rebuilding programme was spectacular but in keeping with the Grand's romantic history. One of the description, and asked for confirmation of the time of the 'meeting'. 'Five o'clock?' she queried. 'But the royal waiters don't come on duty until 7 o'clock!'

'I can't be sure it was a ghost I saw,' Mildred concedes. 'He *looked* real enough, but there hadn't been a matinee that day, and when we checked, neither of the royal waiters had been in the theatre during the afternoon.' If it was a ghost, there are no clues as to whom it might have been.

Finally, perhaps the most spectacular and scary incident happened in 1964 during the preparation for *Camelot*, when two members of the backstage team – John Jordan, then a production electrician and Tony Corbett, a student from Leeds University working at the theatre during the summer vacation – saw something which was not a ghost as we define the term but would certainly have passed for a supernatural force, if only there was some precedent by which to judge it.

At the time, the stage was used constantly during the day for rehearsals, so that most of the technical work had to be done at night. One evening, work could not start until after midnight and in the early hours, only three people were left in the theatre – one of the flymen, in addition to the two electricians already mentioned, were working on a star cloth (ie fitted with an array of fairy lights). The work was slow and painstaking (the one cloth took three nights to complete), and at 5am John and Tony were on stage with the flyman above raising and lowering the cloth to their requirements.

Almost a quarter of a century later, John, now stage manager at the Grand Opera House, Belfast, remembers the incident vividly. 'It was July and pretty warm and we were working in our shirtsleeves,' he recalls. 'The main and safety curtains were up and the cleaners' lights were on in the auditorium, which meant that we had a pretty clear view from the stage. We were preoccupied with what we were doing, but suddenly the atmosphere became icy cold. Obviously the drop in temperature came as a surprise, but perhaps not significant enough to distract us unduly – had it not been for what happened next. Our attention was literally grabbed by a strange roaring noise from the back of the circle – like something between the sound of a rushing wind or gale, and a train hurtling through a tunnel. It was quite alarming, and

31

as we looked up we saw a heavy grey mist floating across the circle, where it seemed to hover. It was the sort of experience – the noise particularly – that makes the hair on your neck stand up, and any instinctive desire to take a closer look was swept aside. I can't say it was a ghost, but it was like nothing I'd seen or heard before or since, and in all these years I've never been able to arrive at a rational explanation; there simply isn't one.'

2

OTHER LIVELY PLAYHOUSES

One of the most bizarre incidents encountered in the course of my researches – something that happened at the much haunted Tameside Theatre, Ashton-under-Lyne, unfortunately comes to you second-hand, because it was experienced by a former manager who has since died. Bert Walsh had the unforgettable experience of passing through an invisible cloud of what could well have been ectoplasm.

The story was relayed to me by the present manager, Jack Clark, who has also had some interesting experiences in his long spell at Tameside, and who is convinced that every detail of his friend and colleague's account the following morning was completely truthful. Mr Walsh, accompanied by a friend, was leaving the building late one night, walking through a darkened auditorium in the direction of backstage and the stage door. As they approached the bottom of the stalls, they heard the strains of a violin playing; it was coming from the stage. In common with most managers who work late, Mr Walsh could see quite well in the dark, and it was apparent there was no one on stage – and he already knew there was nobody else in the theatre. Determined to investigate, he headed in the direction of the music, followed by his companion, but immediately they set foot on stage, it stopped as though the musician had been interrupted. There was nothing to see and ostensibly the illusion, or whatever it had been, was over. Nevertheless, they still had to cross the stage to reach the passage leading to the stage door exit. 'He had only taken a couple of strides when he found he was moving into a clammy tangle of what seemed like elastic cobwebs which not only made it difficult to move, but seemed to clutch at his chest and throat, making it difficult to breathe,' recalled Jack Clark. 'He said it was a terrible experience, making the hairs stand up at the back of his neck. It was a struggle to break through, but having done so he wondered if it had been an hallucination, and said nothing to his companion who had been behind. In the passage he turned on the light switch and saw that his friend was white as a sheet. When, as though he didn't know, he enquired what the matter was he was given a frightening account that matched his own in every respect.'

In fact, Tameside, built in 1900, may well have more than one ghost, because in addition to the violin-playing episode, there have been a number of mysterious incidents, including sightings.

Ten years ago the Lancashire branch of the Society for Psychical Research spent a night at the theatre, installing an infra-red camera and tape recorder in the circle foyer, and others on the stage. It seems unlikely that anything was picked up on film, and typically cautious they were not prepared to discuss their findings, but they did tell Jack Clark that the circle foyer area was 'very active', and when he asked if they had detected the presence of 'Ernie', as the ghostly violin player had become known, they admitted they had picked up a *woman's* voice!

The identity of the ghost(s) is not known, although logic points to two tragic deaths in the building – the first some eighty years ago when the son of a senior police officer hanged himself in the balcony; and the second, in 1934, when the boxes and 'gods' were removed in the process of renovation, and a stagehand hanged himself on stage, allegedly because of financial problems. But if the ghost is of either man, Jack Clark has never had cause to be afraid. 'I've had that ominous tingling in the spine on a number of occasions,' he concedes, 'but I know that whoever it is means me no harm.'

Jack's experiences go back to the days when he was assistant to the former manager. On one occasion he was alone backstage testing the theatre's emergency lighting equipment. Between tests he was sitting, reading a newspaper, in number three dressing room. 'Then I heard bounding footsteps across the stage. I thought it would be the manager coming back to see why some of the lights had been left on, so I decided to frighten him by hiding behind the sliding door to the stage and jumping out on him. When the footsteps were right outside, I slid open the door and leapt out – but there was no one there. Yet as soon as I closed it again, the footsteps started – going back across the stage.'

On two occasions when he was involved in cinema duties the ghost or ghosts were in more mischievous mood. The first time he was sitting on top of the screen after it had been given a re-spray, and the screen began to shake so violently that he almost fell off. Assuming it was caused by the painters below he called down in protest and clung on, but when it continued to shake he managed to climb down, intending to give them a piece of his mind – but they had left the building some time before. On the other occasion he was in the projection box, running the film, and intent on watching the cue marks on the film ready to change reels. His concentration was suddenly disturbed by a tap on the shoulder, and he assumed that it was the projectionist from another cinema with whom he was friendly, and who would often pop in for a chat. 'Give over, Philip,' he exclaimed, and when the tap was repeated, his complaint held more than a note of exasperation. He turned round automatically – but there was nobody there.

Another sighting occurred late one night when he glanced through the glass panels at the sides of the circle foyer doors. There were small posters stuck over the glass so he could only see parts of the person outside, but it was reasonable to suppose it was the 'beat' policeman who often came in at about that time. He called out loudly, 'I'm in here,' but the figure did not respond and began to move away, so he followed him out, catching the back of him going downstairs. The figure still seemed unaware of him and continued down to the downstairs foyer which was pitch black. Jack followed keeping it in sight until it suddenly vanished in the darkness. Having confirmed that all the doors were locked, he knew there was no way a person could have got out of the theatre. By now he was convinced that the intruder was a burglar, but at that moment the policeman did arrive and together they searched the premises from top to bottom. 'Every door was locked so it was impossible for anyone to get in or out,' he maintains.

During the pantomime season in January 1977, the two stars – comedian Jack Douglas, and ventriloquist Keith Harris – were walking across the front of the stalls engaged in conversation when they became conscious of someone beckoning them from the back. It was difficult in the poor light to make out exactly who the person was but they somehow assumed it was Fred, the stage door keeper. They acknowledged that they had seen him and were coming in due course and carried on talking. However, when they saw him beckoning again they headed in his direction, although on arriving at the back of the stalls they realised the man they had kept in vision had either vanished into thin air – or they had walked through him. Jack Clark, near at hand, remembers the incident vividly because Jack Douglas was 'as white as a sheet', although Keith Harris seemed to take it in his stride. Ten years later Keith recalls a shadow-like figure, and admits he was not quite so cool, but that it did not register at first, and the initial reaction was followed by a sense of disbelief.

With dramatic cutbacks in mining and steel industries, South Wales might be regarded as one of Britain's depressed areas. But the city of Swansea supported by timely grants from the EEC was determined not only to survive, but to become a cultural centre for Wales and the West. Symbolic of this ambition was a £7$^1/_2$ million transformation of its famous Grand Theatre into what could ultimately be one of the most impressive arts complexes in Europe. The concept was to blend past and future by building above and around the existing theatre – preserving the original auditorium which has so much charm and character. The first phase, a huge predominantly glass structure, incorporating an enlarged stage area and new fly tower with the latest electronic backstage equipment, was completed a few years ago, although further work continued until 1987.

The Grand offers a six-month repertory season plus pantomime; the rest of the year being open to touring shows – and one of the incentives for embarking on the hugely ambitious project was to offer better facilities to the larger companies on tour. The days are now gone when shoppers were transfixed by the sight of traffic being held up by members of the visiting Welsh National Opera carrying scenery across the road from a make-shift store in the bus station!

The story of the rebuilding programme was spectacular but in keeping with the Grand's romantic history. One of the

oldest touring theatres, opened in 1897 by the celebrated so-
prano Dame Adelina Patti, its many attractions included the
innovative use of electricity to light the stage. The great
Henry Irving appeared here several times; the last only a week
before his death – so that his name-plate on the star dressing
room door is still preserved. Other 'names' include Bransby
Williams, Jessie Matthews, Ivor Novello, Forbes Robertson,
Richard Burton and Mrs Patrick Campbell, surely the only
leading lady to have been involved in a fight with the
stage manager.

Sadly forgotten is a young actress remembered only as Jenny,
who gave her last performance here in 1911 before heading for
America on the *Titanic*. Some say it is her ghost that is most
likely to be the 'White Lady', seen on a number of occasions,
and whose presence is also identified by the scent of violets.
Another popular candidate is Adelina Patti, although the
general demeanour of the Grand's resident ghost would not
seem to conform to that of a very grand lady who would
have been fifty-four by the time she was invited to open the
theatre. However, because of the uncertainty, it is only fair
to draw attention to a third possibility, curiously enough
also drowned.

Eleanor Thomas, currently wardrobe mistress at the
Grand, and a former actress, first saw the resident ghost
when she was playing in *A Street Car Named Desire* in 1972.
While on stage during a performance, something attracted
Eleanor's attention from the dress circle. When she was able
to take a proper look she realised it was a woman dressed
in what was practically a dazzling white – yet even as she
looked, the figure vanished. When she reported the incident
later to Vivyan Ellacott, house manager at the Grand until
1977, she discovered that he had also seen the 'White Lady'.
Coincidentally, that year was the theatre's seventy-fifth anniversary and a commemorative concert included a suitably
appropriate sketch about the ghost of Dame Patti. After the
show, a member of the audience intrigued by the subject of
ghosts approached Eleanor Thomas and told her that his
mother had been a wardrobe mistress at the Grand; that she
had had a premonition of something unexpected happening to
her and announced that if it came true she would come back

to the place she loved – the theatre! In due course she was drowned en route for Ireland, and from then on there were stories of a ghost.

The ghost was quiet when reconstruction work at the theatre was at its height, but when most of the disruption was over, she signalled her return during a performance of the pantomime *Babes In The Wood*. Principal dancer Wendy Weaver, playing the Fairy Godmother, was waiting alone in the wings for her entrance when she felt a hand on her shoulder. She was conscious of a 'presence' at her side, but the touch was cold, and when it was obvious that no one was in touching distance, Wendy admits to having the shivers. But all that happened was that the hand appeared to pull her (and magic wand!) on to the stage. Whether it was an association of ideas or wishful thinking, other members of the cast claimed to have had similar experiences on or about the stage.

When reports of the ghost continued, the local *South Wales Evening Post* decided to conduct an all-night vigil – an assignment undertaken by reporter Antony Harris and photographer Ian Kennedy in February 1984. It was to be an eventful night described by Antony in his report as 'harrowing'. As it happens I had met Antony Harris when he interviewed me about one of my crime novels – and the coincidental connection between me, formerly a journalist on the same newspaper, and my son Duncan who was then company manager for the Grand's repertory programme. I knew him to be a good and colourful writer, so when I began to read his atmospheric report I was a little suspicious. The following passage illustrates the reason for my scepticism:

'The silence is deathly. Every sound assumes nightmare proportions. Every click, every clack, every bump, everything – it is quiet enough to hear a mouse sneeze. My cigarette was lit. I could hear it burning and it sounded like a blast furnace. Every tiny sound carries and is amplified until you just want to clear your dry throat and cry out – shattering the stark air with one human sound . . .'

His throat may have been dry, but one could hardly say the same for his style. However, the account gradually became more factual:

'. . . At 1.20am according to my log, we heard noises in the bar. Bottles clinked together and we both held our breath, but needn't have bothered . . . At 2.25 the temperature dropped savagely and suddenly and for half an hour my eyes and ears strained against the black night. Something was up – I could feel the gooseflesh rising and I shivered involuntarily.

'Then IT happened. A woman began to cry. Softly at first and then with increasing desperation. We both sat bolt upright. We just didn't believe this was happening. Open-mouthed we listened and she stopped. The noise had come from the stage and it was the longest three hours of my life to date. We could hear shuffling footsteps all round us. Random noises became more and more frequent. Then deep beneath us, a harp played. Just one swift run of the fingers along its many strings. It was too weird to be true. Then ever so softly, music played. From whence it came we know not, but it was enough to make my flesh creep. Electronic sounds but no recognisable tune.

'At 5am we took cover in one of the theatre's four boxes and huddled together like children. For the last hour we sat motionless like two stuffed ferrets, our eyes glazed, our mouths dry, and our minds alert despite the lack of sleep. All through this game of cat and mouse we had thought someone was behind all the stunts. We thought we had been set up and looked forward to morning when the 'ghosts' would reveal themselves and share the joke with us. They never did . . .'

In the event, it transpired that someone *had* tried to fool the investigators, but nearly four years later Antony Harris still believed that the woman's sobs and the harp music have no earthly explanation. 'It was a month before one of the electricians admitted that he had managed to conceal himself in the lighting box, and that he had been responsible for certain noises, such as the bottles clinking, but when he had had his fun he left,' Antony concedes. 'He swears that he never left the lighting box above us and we were convinced that if he wasn't just a bit scared to tempt fate by hanging around, he certainly wasn't prepared to waste a night's sleep – having made his point with the bottles.

'As it happens, we hadn't been impressed by his man-made noises – especially after what was to come, and that was much nearer the stage area. Besides, he's a very big fellow with a naturally deep, gruff voice. There is absolutely no way he could have imitated a young woman's sobs, and we know for certain that no one was with him.'

Shortly after the all-night vigil, a local medium offered to use his special powers to identify the ghost. Amidst considerable ballyhoo he held a seance on stage, accompanied by three members of the Swansea Psychic Centre. But his claims to have been contacted – not by the 'White Lady' – but by Welsh comedian Ryan Davies who had starred at the Grand many times, and who had died in America in 1977, lacked any credibility.

At yet another seance organised by TV AM, the claims of a different professional medium were far more modest, and in that sense possibly more impressive. No hint of direct contact with the spirit world, but of a definite ghostly *presence* in the dress circle. Although the medium could not have known, it was very near the spot where Eleanor Thomas had first seen the 'White Lady' in 1972. Little more, perhaps, than another tiny piece of the jigsaw, but the problem with well-publicised seances is that the more spectacular claims are remembered and doubts conveniently forgotten, thus adding to the self-perpetuating local folklore. In fact, romantic though she is, there is no real evidence of a visible ghost at the Grand, although perhaps enough material to give the 'White Lady' the benefit of the doubt!

The question with 'Henry', the Oldham Coliseum resident ghost, is not so much whether he exists – more whether it is a possible case of mistaken identity. Henry's story is dramatic – not to say 'theatrical' – so it has been natural to assume that he was responsible for all the paranormal activity over the past forty years. But there is reason to believe that the considerable activity there may have been shared with at least one other spirit.

The Coliseum today is one of the country's most interesting repertory companies, commissioning a relatively high number of original plays. However, its drama tradition is quite short, with its origins actually in circus. If that sounds novel then what makes it unique is that it was virtually 'rejected' at birth. Its strange story began in 1885 when local businessman, Thomas Whittaker, built a wood-constructed arena for a large American circus, and when the money did not materialise he was stuck with it. Being a man of initiative, Whittaker leased the wooden showplace to various circuses, and used it for a period as a ballroom and eventually a music hall. However, when he discovered its potential as a theatre, licensing problems caused him to look for another site – and this turned out to be just as unusual – over a filled-in reservoir by the approach to Holebottom Colliery which had ceased operating only a few years before. Although the design was very different, Whittaker had the Grand Circus dismantled and sections (specially fire-proofed) used in the new construction. It was named Colosseum.

Under new ownership, in 1912 the Colosseum became a cinema, although variety acts continued to share the bill, and despite the fact that plays and pantomime were later introduced it became a full-time cinema in 1931, at a time when talkies revitalised that business. But this success was shortlived and the building was closed for seven years. The future of Oldham theatre was at last guaranteed by a group of local enthusiasts who wanted their own repertory company, and the Playgoers Club which had developed an impressive membership eventually reopened the derelict theatre shortly before the onset of World War II. In the 1950s it was extensively rebuilt, but in common with most theatres around the country, TV was causing audiences to shrink, and in 1978 the town council were obliged to take over.

'Henry' is generally assumed to be the ghost of an actor, Harold Norman, who died in 1947 after a stage fight went wrong during a production of Macbeth. Since no-one denies that Macbeth courts disaster – the name is seldom spoken, being referred to as The Scottish Play – obvious conclusions were drawn. At the climax of the play, Macbeth and Macduff fight a duel interspersed with appropriate dialogue, leaving the stage locked in mortal combat. The audience does not see the fatal thrust and only discovers the outcome when Macduff returns carrying the head of the vanquished. However, in the Coliseum's 1947 production the carefully staged fight might have been more realistic than usual (or badly rehearsed) because it culminated in Macduff's dagger, supposed to pierce the cloak, finding a different target – Harold Norman's stomach. In some ways it might have been an actor's dream,

except that Shakespeare had not prepared a death scene, and the visibly wounded Norman crawled to the side of the stage and the curtain was brought down.

Exciting stuff! In fact, such a good story, I am reluctant to add the sobering news that Norman died in hospital four weeks later from acute peritonitus, and that police had already announced that the stab wound was superficial and had been accidental. However, this did not stop rumours that there had been bad feeling between the duellists, and that even if it had been accidental, it had certainly been a direct consequence of the bad luck that comes automatically with the play. The accident happened on a Thursday night, and needless to say, most of the reported happenings have been on a Thursday! An interesting footnote is that in 1988, the Coliseum premiered a play, *Stage Fright*, they had commissioned from Peter Fieldson and 'inspired' by the 1947 mishap. It featured a murder in a repertory production of *Macbeth* and the consequences.

The individual who has encountered the supernatural in one form or another might be accused by cynics of suffering from an overheated imagination. But animals are not prone to hallucinations – at least, not about ghosts – and there are dozens of cases where cats and dogs, especially guard dogs used on night security duties, have been scared by something unseen, and not apparent to the people who accompanied them. At the Coliseum there have been at least two examples. The first, some years ago, was a little Yorkshire terrier owned by the wardrobe mistress. The terrier virtually lived in the place and yet on certain days would refuse to enter the wardrobe department; not a matter of disobedience but of terror, with teeth bared and its fur standing on end. The behaviour was repeated some years later when the stage manager's dog was brought to the theatre to play a role in a current production. The dog behaved impeccably on and off stage until one day it decided it could not face something in the stage manager's office. No fleeting mood, but something traumatic. Next day the room was normal again, but exactly a week later, the same performance was repeated. The 'no-go' days were Thursdays, of course.

Actual sightings by humans, unfortunately, have been infrequent. The clearest was in 1979 when a designer working late at night on stage glanced up casually into the auditorium and saw a man in a grey polo-neck jumper sprawled in the front row of the dress circle. As there should not have been anyone there, he did a 'double-take' and the man vanished. (The incident is described further on.) A year earlier, former box office manager, Ann Beaumont, called in on a Sunday morning when she was supposed to be meeting a friend nearby. Her friend was not at the arranged meeting point so she returned to the theatre to find the scenery dock doors open; they had been closed when she left shortly before. She went in and through to the foyer – in time to see a shadowy figure going upstairs. The 'texture' made it immediately obvious that it was not a live person, and she screamed and ran out.

During the refurbishing work shortly afterwards one of the decorators was also given a fright when working all night, accompanied only by the caretaker, Ted Blunt, who was sitting at the back of the dress circle. When the workman

43

suddenly demanded to know what he was 'playing at', Ted went over to him and was informed by a visibly shaken companion that the door between them had suddenly swung open and a shadowy figure appeared.

At this stage I must introduce a rival candidate for the identity of the Coliseum ghost. In the 1950s when the theatre ran a weekly rep, the set was dismantled on Sunday morning and the new one built during that day. At that time the carpenter lived in Halifax in West Yorkshire which meant it was impracticable to travel home and be back for an 8am start. In the circumstances he was in the habit of sleeping in the fly gallery. But on one occasion the designer and stage management team arrived on Sunday to find no sign of him. However, when Clive Pickerell had reason to go up into the fly gallery, he found the carpenter hanging. Since there has only been one brief three-dimensional image of the resident ghost, it would be irresponsible to comment on whether 'Henry' was an actor, or a carpenter, which certainly doesn't sound so romantic, or whether they are both still 'tied' to the theatre. What may be more to the point is the fact that the area of the fly gallery where the hanging took place is always very cold, and is adjacent to what were then dressing rooms, but now wardrobe, where 'happenings' have occurred.

Caroline McCullough, now with the Bolton Octagon, was head of design at the Coliseum between 1978 and 1981 during which she had a couple of experiences which may not be 'hard' evidence, but are certainly difficult to explain away. The first was when she had only been there for a few months; she and two colleagues were in the paint shop working all night on some scenery. In the early hours, the electricians called by to say they were leaving, locking up behind them. At 3am the design team were engrossed in painting when the room's internal phone rang. Caroline admits that because the call was so unexpected and they knew there was no one in the building it was some time before any of them reacted positively, and by the time she answered the extension there was no one at the other end. However, just in case there was someone in the building trying to contact them, Caroline hovered near the extension – and when it rang again she was able to answer it fairly promptly; but again the line was dead. When it rang a third time she was standing nearby and literally pounced on the receiver, but silence – not even heavy breathing! Having established it was no prank, none of the technicians could come up with a rational explanation.

What happened a couple of years later *could* have been a case of auto-suggestion, she concedes, but while I believe in the power of mass hypnosis in certain conditions, I am not sure about the effect of suggestion on the consciousness of two very different personalities, thinking independently of each other. It was another Sunday all-nighter, and her companion was another designer, Robert Jones. 'I must admit that on this occasion we were tempting fate,' Caroline told me. 'Robert hadn't long been with us and asked what it was like working all night, and I somewhat facetiously made some remark about it being no problem if we weren't interrupted by the ghost. So I suppose the seeds of fear might have been planted at that stage.'

Caroline and Robert finished their painting by about 1.30 am. Because of the positioning of the light switches, anyone leaving has to cross the stage area in darkness, and by then it had suddenly become quite 'spooky'. The exit is through an internal stage door solidly built because of the proximity of a theatre bar from which sounds might otherwise be heard on stage. 'Because of its weight, it took quite an effort to pull the door open,' Caroline explained. 'It also has a very distinct creaking noise. But when it was open, Robert, in a rather childish fit of bravado called out: "We're going now . . . Goodbye!" The door closed behind us and we were in a narrow corridor with the door to the bar on our left, and the crash doors to the street on our right. In the darkness I was suddenly disorientated and shut the crash doors in the wrong order. When I eventually got it right, I couldn't turn the key in the lock. While I was fiddling with the lock I heard the very distinctive sound of the internal stage door creak as it was pulled open. The door was far too heavy to have been blown open – it had to be pulled, and even that took some effort. Nor was it any other sound, because the crash doors had settled down and it was perfectly quiet apart from the sound of my key scrabbling about in the lock. At that stage I probably panicked and thrust the key in Robert's hand, and he managed to turn it in the lock, after which I felt a bit easier. Then he asked if *I* had heard the internal door creak, and we hurried off – with me trying to keep up with him!'

In 1979 there was so much paranormal activity that members of the stage management team took it upon themselves to hold a series of seances using a ouija board – and coming to the conclusion that there were two or even three ghosts on the premises. Alan Nield, having recently returned to the Coliseum as production manager, was then a DSM and remembers joining in the seances with a great deal of scepticism, but gradually changing his attitude because of the results achieved. He points out that the circle was not always made up of the same people, so there was no question of anyone controlling the board. 'On one occasion we were in contact with a man who said he had been run over by a horse and cart on a right-of-way that used to be outside the theatre,' Alan told me. 'At that time none of us knew the history of the theatre, but in due course we were able to check everything from the records.'

There were a number of interesting 'messages' received from these sessions, but undoubtedly the most dramatic aftermath was during a production of Shaw's *Saint Joan* when a heavy snowfall caused the cancellation of an evening performance. With a number of staff in the theatre at a loose end, the psychic 'explorers' decided to have another seance on stage. Alan Nield recalls the occasion: 'There was nothing particularly memorable about the actual seance, except that we knew it was a theatrical person – probably Harold Norman – because of the technical terms he used, such as "raise the iron" (safety curtain) which had been dropped. We finished at about 9.30 and when we left I locked up. Next day I had to be first in, and when I arrived at the stage door I noticed some white powder seemed to be "bleeding" from under the door.' The powder was incense which is burned during the play (charcoal in containers being heated, rather like a barbecue, and the powder sprinkled on to create the smell; when the containers are waved about smoke is produced).

'Inside, the whole floor was covered with the chalk-like dust, and the stage was in a mess with the burners smashed – as though they had been thrown against the wall. All the charcoal had been crushed, as though each piece had been individually squeezed into black dust.'

On another occasion during the intense spell of paranormal activity, Alan was on stage with Steven Selwyn (now at the Mayfair theatre in London) and Robert Jones, the designer mentioned earlier. They were painting scenery, with all the stage lights on, but those in the auditorium off. Suddenly they were distracted by the sound of all the doors in the auditorium blowing open – simultaneously. 'We didn't say anything, but each of us was conscious of a strange light in the openings,' Alan recalls, 'far from being scared, we all had the same thought – that someone had got into the building and was playing a joke on us. So we took off as one, in different directions – one to the dress circle, the others downstairs – but we were wrong; there was no one about!'

It was Robert Jones, now at the Nottingham Playhouse, who saw the ghost in the dress circle. Again it was during a fit-up late at night, and the auditorium was in darkness. He has never forgotten the experience, although it did not worry him at the time. 'First I was conscious of a door in the circle opening and someone crossing through the seats. I was busy and didn't pay too much attention but when I did look up again, it was by instinct, and there was a man in a grey polo-necked jumper sprawled in a seat in the front row. He was wearing green wellington boots raised up as though he was very much at home. It was a surprise, and in the time it took to do a "double-take" he vanished. On describing him later, I was told that had been the way the carpenter who hanged himself used to dress – and that was the first I had heard of someone dying.' Could it have been imagination, or association of ideas? Robert cannot be sure but it seems unlikely. 'I can't remember exactly what I was thinking about all those years ago, but I know I was busy and concentrating on what I was doing, so I'm reasonably sure I wasn't daydreaming of ghosts.'

The cynic might question the 'reliability' of the people whose experiences I have quoted, but I would point out that over the years they have all worked at a number of differ-ent theatres but nowhere else have any of them come across anything untoward. In their view the Coliseum is unique.

Incidentally, adjoining the theatre is what was once the

Temperance Hall – used by the initial repertory company in the 1930s while waiting for the Coliseum to be renovated – which in recent years has been used as carpenters' workshops, and store for the sets. The Temperance Hall seems to have its own ghost which, according to the carpenters who work there, comes and goes over the Christmas season. Former master carpenter, Donald Shortland, believes that someone committed suicide in an adjoining house (where the props are now stored), but that the ghost appears to have something in common with them because when they have been putting sets together he has heard a mystery banging which has carried on sometimes long after they stopped, but was definitely not an echo. But his former assistant, Simon Dalton, now in charge of props at BBC-TV in Manchester, had some unnerving experiences soon after he joined the Coliseum in 1979. While working he was tapped twice on the shoulder – quite firmly – and when he turned round no one was there. 'It was the same evening that I saw the figure of a middle-aged man standing in the doorway to the old house,' he told me. 'I realised it couldn't have been a real person, because the house was empty and the only entrance was through the Temperance Hall where I was working. It was only there for a second or two before disappearing, but it was suddenly cold and I was quite unnerved.'

3

STAR BILLING

In an age when the accolade 'star' is bestowed so readily that mediocre performers can be elevated to top billing by a massive but indiscriminate TV audience, even the true star no longer stands out. There are now so many successful artistes competing for our attention we might be excused for forgetting the relatively few really bright stars of yesterday.

Theatre enthusiasts will recognise names such as David Garrick, Edmund Kean, Sarah Siddons, and Sarah Bernhardt but even they might be stumped by that of William Terriss (1847–97), for example, who was once affectionately known as 'Breezy Bill', or 'No 1, Adelphi Terriss', after the theatre with which he was mainly associated, the Adelphi in the Strand. Terriss, strikingly handsome, and with much of the charisma of the younger Olivier, succeeded in a variety of roles from Romeo and Nicholas Nickleby to heroes in a series of swashbuckling melodramas – the equivalent of today's soap operas. His popularity was further boosted by the apparent integrity of his private life, and for his personal courage, kindness and generosity to fellow actors. However, it was the manner of his death at the age of fifty that earned his greatest headlines – being murdered outside the theatre that meant so much to him. His ghost has been in evidence ever since.

It was only nine days before Christmas 1897 that Terriss who had been starring in the box office success, *Secret Service*, was stabbed by an insanely jealous and unsuccessful actor, Richard Prince, known as 'Mad Archer' (Prince being a stage name). Prince had brooded for some time over the leading man's constant success, while he was still overlooked and persecuted by the acting establishment. Finally, having reached the end of his tether, and convinced that the only solution to his problem was Terriss's death, he laid in wait for him by the stage door before an evening performance. As Terriss fumbled for the key to his special pass-door, Prince leapt out of the shadows and stabbed him three times with a kitchen knife. Mortally wounded, Terriss staggered inside and, as any great actor would wish, had time to make his farewell speech as he bled to death in the arms of his leading lady (and mistress), Jessie Milward. 'I will come back', were the prophetic words imprinted on her memory. By the time he breathed his last, some twenty minutes later, there had been another slice of pure drama from his famous son-in-law, Seymour Hicks (the actor-dramatist, who had formed the ideal partnership with Terriss's daughter, Ellaline, and who was subsequently knighted) who was to claim that in the hushed atmosphere he heard a disembodied voice proclaim: 'Are there men living such fools as to think there is no hereafter?'

Incidentally, in Joseph Braddock's *Haunted Houses* (Batsford 1956), there is an intriguing footnote to the murder. Terriss's understudy, a mime artist called Lane, had a premonition of the murder on the night before it happened. In his dream he saw Terriss bleeding to death inside the theatre, surrounded by his friends – Lane among them. But when he repeated his nightmare as a warning, everyone laughed at him, and the stabbing occurred exactly as he had seen it in his dream, with himself in exactly the same position.

The evidence over the years undoubtedly leans towards the presence of some aspect of the supernatural, although many of the reports of ghostly phenomena – peculiar 'tapping' noises coming from the star's former dressing room, are the sort of sounds that occur quite naturally in many large old buildings, and so should be discounted without supporting evidence – which is difficult to come by with incidents that happened half a century ago, with all the 'witnesses' having since died. Similarly, reports that a ghostly figure answering the description of Terriss in the way he used to dress, had been seen by London Transport staff at Covent Garden underground station, have got out of hand. Initial reports were, at least, impressive; then they began to grow – still feasible since they occurred once a year in December to coincide with the murder. But recently I heard a ticket collector on radio declare that he saw the ghost of William Terriss 'most nights'! If that is the case, then the actor must spend far more time in the station than he does in the theatre to which he is supposed to be tied.

The existing deceptively large theatre (1,500 seats) which opened in 1930 with a succession of C. B. Cochran musicals – a tradition which has been maintained to this day – is the fourth on the site. The first (1806), called the Sans Pareil, was little more than a showcase for the talents of the owner's daughter whose one-woman act concluded with a display of fireworks! It was renamed the Adelphi in 1819 when the programme generally consisted of adaptations of the novels of Sir Walter Scott and melodramas – a precedent which may well have inspired the successful Terriss formula over seventy years later.

Mr T. L. W. Porter (known as 'Bill' in the business) executive director of the Adelphi for many years until his retirement in the 1980s, still retains an open mind on the supernatural because he has not seen anything that was in his view totally convincing. 'Undoubtedly, some people have had some strange

Interior of the New Adelphi Theatre

experiences,' he concedes. 'We once had a fireman who fled after just one night and said he wasn't coming back – he was too scared to even talk about it! Another who had a dog which wouldn't go past one of the ladies' toilets. He would stop several feet away, and "freeze", hackles up, in a state of terror – and no amount of coercion would drag him past that door. I can vouch for the fact that there is a distinct chill in that area. We also had reports from maintenance men of freak incidents such as the lift going up and down for no apparent reason, and once in the upper circle the seats in a complete row began to tip up and down in sequence like legs in a chorus line.'

But other reports sensationalised at the time, are discounted by Bill Porter, who cautiously puts some of his own experiences into context; eg at times he has seen 'something' moving at the back of the stalls; at other times objects in his office had 'disappeared'. 'I *thought* I'd seen something. They could have been ghostly manifestations; equally they could have been conjured up by my imagination. Similarly, things could have disappeared simply because my memory was playing tricks. It's far too easy to jump to romantic conclusions.'

However, Mr Porter's former assistant, Jim Myers, then house manager at the Adelphi and now at the Whitehall Theatre, has more positive memories, including a rare sighting. Ostensibly the most dramatic occurred in 1983 during a run of *Marilyn* (based on the Marilyn Monroe story) when the star, Stephanie Lawrence, gave a party for the cast in honour of her understudy who had taken over the lead in a matinee performance. Surprising though it may seem, there is a real risk in all large theatres after a show of people – perhaps going to a toilet – getting lost and even being locked in for the night. Since there were guests not familiar with the building, the company manager actually made a special announcement to those at the party in the royal circle, that all doors other than in the main front foyer would be locked, and that it was essential they remember to leave by the front.

As the party started at about 11pm when the stage door keeper had left, the duty fireman was instructed to remain in the stage door area to redirect anyone who still managed to lose their bearings; someone was also delegated to cover the front foyer to prevent anyone coming in from the street.

Occupied with various odd jobs, Jim Myers did not attend the party; nor did he drink anything in his office. Like most theatre parties when people have had a long day, it began to break up after an hour or so, and everyone had gone by the time Mr Myers made his final check-up round at 12.45. The only people in the building were the fireman, still in the stage door area, and the theatre electrician at front of house. Every door was locked and going downstairs, Jim had to unlock the double gates into the back of the stalls (locking them again behind him) and follow his usual instinctive pattern, turning right along the back row to the end gangway and down towards the stage, in order to cross behind to the stage door. The emergency lights left on for the cleaners ensured that he could see quite clearly, and with a taxi booked for a few minutes' time, his stride was purposeful.

He was looking ahead when, about three or four rows down he noticed in the corner of his vision a tall dark figure standing in the opposite corner, ie the front row of the stalls by the far end of the orchestra pit. His spontaneous reaction was that it was the fireman who had disobeyed instructions and left his post at the stage door, but was already dismissing the notion when the man failed to react in character. An almost simultaneous thought was that the man was an 'idiot' from the party who despite the warnings, had managed to lose himself.

Trying to recognise the tall figure, Jim Myers cut across the seats to the centre gangway, calling out: 'This way out! Can you come over here?' When there was no response, he added: 'Who is it?' Years later he remembers the incident clearly. 'At that point, although I could see quite well, I began to have certain doubts. Initially, I was quite certain it was a masculine shape; then I blinked in case my eyes were playing tricks because suddenly it could have been a woman. The more my eyes strained to identify the figure, the less positive the features were, almost blurred, like a distorted television picture.

'In order to concentrate I had stopped; then, as I watched, it seemed to step up into the air – there were no steps, only the orchestra pit wall which was waist high, which wasn't feasible – then on to the corner of the stage. I was still puzzling that out when it vanished.'

Mr Myers maintains that he was not alarmed in any way; in fact, perfectly cool. He waited for the sound of footsteps on the stage or any other sound, but heard nothing, so carried on to the front of the stalls then diagonally across the stage – but found no sign of the mystery figure. By now, he suspected it might have been a ghost, and would have welcomed any further sign or clue to its presence, such as a drop in temperature – but he found nothing. Having met and 'cross-examined' Jim Myers, I am reasonably certain he did not imagine the incident.

Jim Myers does not claim any psychic powers, but he had a number of interesting experiences during his spell at the Adelphi. In 1984 there were two. The first, which amused the night staff, he did not take very seriously. Sitting in his office late one night, he heard footsteps in the corridor outside. They stopped outside his door, and the handle was turned. He got up to see who it was, but there was no one there. Having checked with the other members of the night staff, it was evident that none of them had been anywhere near his office. Even so, it did not concern him unduly and the mystery was relegated to the back of his mind. However, a second incident several weeks later was rather more sinister. He had stayed particularly late to feed box office takings and other statistics into the computer. Everyone had gone, except the duty fireman in his room, and the theatre was completely locked. It was very quiet when suddenly he heard footsteps, apparently going downstairs. When they stopped just as suddenly, he reconsidered; perhaps the sound had come from outside in the street, silent at that time of night.

Ten minutes later, the footsteps began again. He then heard a door open at the end of the corridor – he was able to identify it from its distinctive creaking sound, and then the men's toilet door opened. Believing it could only have been the fireman, he dialled his number on the in-house phone system, but his colleague answered immediately. His reaction was one of amusement, recalling the previous incident but when he realised that Jim was in earnest, he replied. 'No, I *really* haven't been up there! Maybe I should come up?'

Jim was still holding the phone when he heard an outside door slam. 'At that moment I *knew* something was wrong. It could have been a burglar, or more than one, who had broken in through a door on the roof. Then my own door which had been slightly open slammed shut very violently; a heavy door which would not have been affected by draught.

'As I shouted "Who's there!?" another door slammed and down the phone I heard "I'm coming up!" In fact, the fireman was up in a flash, a baton in his hand, expecting to find intruders. We searched the building from top to bottom, expecting to find signs of entry, particularly from the roof – but every door was locked and every bolt still intact. It was obvious that no one could have got in – or out.'

Jim Myers remains mystified. 'How can I say with confidence it was a ghost? Especially when one wonders what a ghost would want with a toilet, but then who knows what was in that area before? Certainly part of it was once used as a storeroom. All I know is that I didn't imagine those footsteps, yet there was definitely no one else in the vicinity, and the doors slamming were violent enough to be heard at the other end of the phone.'

There are other more dramatic stories which I have been unable to substantiate because they happened so long ago, such as one of a musical comedy actress who, in 1928, used the dressing room traditionally reserved for the leading lady. Apparently she did not know of the Terriss legend; nor that the star used to knock twice on his leading lady's door with his walking stick to let her know he had arrived. One day, between matinee and evening performances, the actress lay down on a couch for a rest – until an unseen force began to shake it violently. Then she felt her arm gripped as though to get her attention, and then a greenish light hovering in front of the dressing table mirror. When she reached out for it, the light vanished – but the bruises on her arm were real enough! It was only then that she heard two distinct taps on the door, although it transpired no one was outside.

The only 'corroboration' of something strange about No one dressing room (now an office), is from Jim Myers who, shortly after his arrival at the Adelphi when the theatre was 'dark' between plays, decided to take a nap in the infamous dressing

room. The attraction was a large bed which befitting a top
star had been bought for Lena Horne during her spell at the
theatre. Having told someone where he would be, he went
to lie down. However, he found it impossible to relax, let
alone sleep. 'The atmosphere was what I can only describe as
unwelcoming, and there was a steady and persistent sound of
tapping throughout the room,' Jim recalls. 'It was a Saturday
afternoon and nothing was happening; there were no workmen
on site and it was not the water pipes – the central heating
was off. I had no reason to be scared, but there was something
not *right* about the place, so I eventually gave up trying to
doze and came out. When I told someone, they laughed at my
innocence – and that was the first I had ever heard about
the legend.' On the other hand, the same dressing room was
used by a number of leading actresses. As far as I have been
able to ascertain, none of them complained to management.

Entering the impressive modern foyer, one might forget
that the Theatre Royal, Bristol, is the oldest theatre in
the country in almost continuous use. It opened in 1766, and
although the modernisation programme nearly two hundred
years later transformed it into a complex, with a new studio
theatre, the original auditorium remains basically the same.
The theatre has always been a trend-setter in drama and now,
as the home of the Bristol Old Vic, its role includes the development of fresh young talent from the drama school linked
with Bristol University.

Reports of at least two ghosts are inspired by a series of
strange incidents over the years. Before an electronic alarm
system was installed, the building was patrolled at night by
a security guard whose Alsatian dogs were often scared of
certain areas, and if released would take flight! The more
publicised ghost is that of Sarah Siddons, who starred there
between 1778–82. The other is believed to be that of a scenic
artist who was killed in the paint dock when the handle of
the paint frame hoist hit him in the face.

The apparition of a woman in costume has been seen
on a number of occasions – the most intriguing on a
night in 1984 when the security guard, Tony Dunn, had
stopped in the auditorium to take a leisurely look at new
gold leaf work on the ceiling. Conscious of being watched

he glanced in the direction of the stage and saw a woman and child by the safety curtain. Mr Dunn claims he recognised Sarah Siddons and her daughter Sally, and spoke her name, but as he approached the figures apparently 'melted' into the curtain. He then hurried backstage but they had vanished. Curiously, he never spoke of the experience, fearing he would be ridiculed, until long after his retirement when the manager John Symonds contacted him on my behalf.

After a royal gala performance in November 1982, in the presence of the Prince of Wales, *four* of the cast standing on stage of the empty theatre became aware of a figure moving across the back of the gallery. But when someone pointed out that the gallery was closed, the figure disappeared. Inconclusive, perhaps, but in the following March during rehearsals, one of the actors on stage was disconcerted by the sight of a costumed lady in the box above the royal box. During the 'fit-up' for the same play (*The Table of the Two Horsemen*), the scenic artist, Jane Cooke, was working through the night on stage when suddenly two of the tube lamps near the flies began to swing violently backwards and forwards for no reason, while a third downstage did not move at all. After forty-five minutes of unexplained movement, Jane was sufficiently unnerved to leave the theatre. No one was ever able to provide an explanation.

In the vicinity of the accident in the old paint dock there have been suggestions from different people of a ghostly 'presence', while Jane Cooke has actually seen the figure of a man wearing a brown sleeveless jerkin. After an electric hoist had been installed, it started up on its own, with no one in reach of the switches – leading to speculation that the ghost had been testing the new equipment!

The imposing 1,500 seat Palace Theatre in Cambridge Circus, London, is perhaps best known for its succession of hit musicals which is perhaps not so surprising because when built in 1891 it was intended as an opera house. Despite its initial impact under the D'Oyly Carte management it became an equally successful Palace of Varieties at which Mistinguette made her London debut, as did Anna Pavlova. The royal command variety performance, now associated with the Palladium, was first held here in 1911.

The ghost most identified with the theatre is, in fact, that of Pavlova, but with remarkably little justification, and I have tried very hard to find someone who has seen or 'felt' her presence – but without success. It is very hard to dent an established legend and such stories often gain credibility because of assumptions which are not checked. Typical is one story which was squashed by the cool head of Eric Willett, chief electrician, who joined the Palace staff thirty-three years ago and who may well be the longest service employee in the West End (although he cannot compete with a former stage door keeper, Charles, who was at the Palace for forty-seven years!). Soon after coming to the Palace, Eric was doing his nightly rounds switching off the house lights on all five levels, working his way down from the gallery. When he reached the back of the stalls and turned off the remaining lights, the house was in darkness and suddenly he became aware of the eerie sound of a cello playing an air from 'The Dying Swan' in the ballet which had become synonymous with Pavlova. Knowing the story, another man might have fled, but using his torch, Eric made his way to the front of the stalls in the direction of the music. In the orchestra pit he found one of the musicians in total darkness playing a cello. 'What did you put the lights out for,' he complained. 'I bought this from a friend tonight, and I couldn't wait to try it out!' But for Eric's down-to-earth curiosity the legend would have been embellished – with Pavlova probably even dancing to ghostly music . . .

In any case, if there is a ballerina ghost, it certainly was not Pavlova if a certain medium is to be believed. The theatre does not have a No 13 dressing room, and in a major variety production in 1958 No 12a was occupied by Petula Clark's accompanist. When he returned after the first night's performance he found the room in a mess, with his personal belongings strewn all over the place. When he reported the matter to the stage door keeper (the long-serving Charles) he was advised that it was standard practice to lock the door, and that he should keep the key with him. Next night the pianist did as he was told – and was even more shocked when later he unlocked the door to find the room in utter chaos again. After this, management moved him to another dressing room where his belongings were left untouched. Although no explanation was forthcoming, one of the stagehands visited a spiritualist who conducted a seance, and told him that the ghost was that of a former ballet dancer who had been jilted by her lover and developed a hatred for men – which meant that female occupants of her dressing room (No 12a) were unmolested, but woe betide any man!

Another legendary 'star' ghost claimed by the theatre is that of Ivor Novello, who died in 1951 during the long run here of his last musical *King's Rhapsody*, and was said to have a special affection for the place. The late impresario, Emile Littler, a confirmed spiritualist, told Eric Willett many years ago that he was in 'regular contact' with Novello, who continued to watch successive shows from a seat in the back row of the dress circle. Since Mr Littler is also now dead it is impossible to elaborate on what other messages he may have received, but a number of sightings of *someone* have been reported in the dress circle – perhaps the most spectacular when auditions were conducted here in 1980 for the Drury Lane production of *Sweeney Todd*. The house was in darkness, with a handful of people from the production sitting in the stalls and the upper levels empty. One of the male singers broke off in the middle of his routine to complain that it was impossible for him to concentrate while 'that chap' was moving across the dress circle all the time. Since the circle was supposed to be empty, Eric Willett was dispatched upstairs to remove whoever it was disturbing the audition. But by the time he arrived, the apparition which could still be seen from the stage during the time it took for him to get there, had vanished.

However, perhaps the most impressive sighting was at a matinee performance during the six-year run of *The Sound of Music* when most of the principals in the cast were somewhat awed by the unexpected presence of a man, resplendent in a scarlet-lined cloak, sitting in the royal box. At the end of the first act several of them enquired the identity of the VIP who was honouring them with his presence – but front of house insisted that the box was empty. When Eric Willett passed on the visitor's description, he was told by the then house manager that it did not make sense because he had given a remarkable likeness of long since dead manager, Charles Morton, who had succeeded to the D'Oyly Carte managership!

4

HISTORY COMES ALIVE

One of the more elegant parts of London's West End lies in the narrow strip between Piccadilly Circus and Buckingham Palace, so it is appropriate that two of the most beautiful theatres – not only in London but in the whole country – should have a royal association and be situated opposite each other in the Haymarket, which runs between the Circus and Pall Mall. They are Her Majesty's and the Theatre Royal, although in common with the other Theatre Royal it is better known for its location, and usually called The Haymarket. Both have a distinguished ghost, and in view of the illustrious history of both theatres, it is perhaps surprising they do not claim more.

The Haymarket is the second oldest London theatre still in use – the original playhouse erected in 1720 and lasting for exactly a century, before being replaced by the present magnificent Nash building. An early licensee was Henry Fielding who used it to produce many of his own plays. There were inevitable rumours of the theatre being haunted by Fielding's ghost, but these were never substantiated.

The playhouse was granted its royal patent in unusual circumstances. It had been taken over in 1747 by actor-playwright Samuel Foote, whose personal talents as a mimic made him a celebrity over the next two decades. However, at a high society party he was the victim of a practical joke in which he was mounted on a horse which, it transpired, was known to be dangerous. Foote was thrown, and a leg broken in the fall subsequently had to be amputated. Since one of the perpetrators was the Duke of York, friends appeased guilty consciences by asking the King to grant his special patent; hence its new name in 1767. However, as its Drury Lane namesake also discovered to its cost, royal patronage could be something of a mixed blessing. In February 1794, its first royal command performance was such an attraction that it was much more than a normal 'House Full' – fifteen people were trampled to death in the crush, and many more injured.

The new theatre which opened in 1821 with Sheridan's *The Rivals* has had a more sober history, albeit more distinguished in the classical sense, with some of the outstanding productions coming from the management of John Buckstone between 1853 and 1865 during which the American actor Edwin Booth (an excellent actor, but probably better known as the brother of the man who assassinated President Lincoln), and Herbert Beerbohm (taking over in 1887) whose own acting career reached a peak with his performance as Svengali in *Trilby*, by George Du Maurier.

It was John Buckstone who stayed on at the Haymarket after his death in 1879, at the age of seventy-seven, after an association lasting more than thirty years (dating from 1833 when he became a successful actor, before taking over the running of the theatre). The first sighting was within a year of his death, and a ghostly apparition fitting Buckstone's description has been seen by a number of people in the past century.

Anthony Peek, who joined the Haymarket as artistic director in 1960, becoming managing director during the next quarter of a century, has seen nothing yet remains convinced of Buckstone's benevolent presence. 'I suspect I'm just not psychic,' he told me. 'In fact, my association goes back a further thirteen years when I was with H. M. Tennant and we staged our productions there. Yet in all those years I never encountered anything that could be regarded as proof of his existence. There were dozens of strange incidents – lights being switched on and off, doors rattling and things disappeared, but nothing that could not have a rational explanation.

'However, I do believe that he loved the theatre very much. He was a tremendous personality, and although he became a little deaf towards the end, and that made him a little irritable, he was held in great affection by all who had known him. People of that stature leave their mark on a place.'

Those who claimed to have seen the ghost of Buckstone during Mr Peek's spell at the Haymarket included the distinguished actress Margaret Rutherford, who played there in *School for Scandal*, and is remembered for a number of eccentric roles, such as the larger-than-life medium in *Blithe Spirit*. 'She lived in Gerrards Cross,' he recalls. 'One night in 1963 it was extremely foggy and it would have been very difficult to get home, so she and her husband (the actor, Stringer Davis) stayed the night. The next day she reported having seen a ghost. I have no doubt she genuinely believed she had seen Buckstone, but I found what she described difficult to swallow from what we know of the man, and I suspected she had been dreaming.'

Subsequently Ms Rutherford reported her experience in an issue of *Psychic News*, in which she described seeing a man's hairy leg through an open cupboard door, after which she saw his face and recognised him as Buckstone. However, this was slightly different from the account she gave Mr Peek only a few hours after the experience. 'She said she first saw his hairy leg, and described his clothes and manner, and although she did not recognise his face we assumed it might

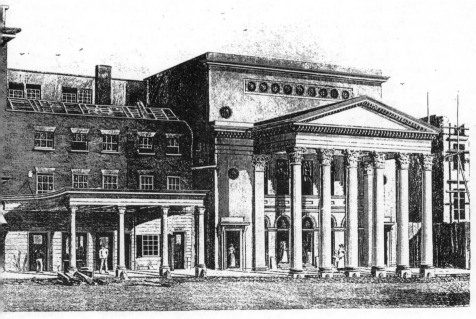

View of the Theatre Royal, Haymarket

have been the actor-manager. But Buckstone was far too much of a gentleman to have appeared in a lady's boudoir in a state of undress, or at least with legs undraped. If she had been dreaming and awoke somewhat dazed, it seems more likely that the leg belonged to her husband; at least, that was my impression.'

In the same year the double-act of Michael Flanders, in his wheelchair, and Donald Swann were appearing on stage in A Drop of Another Hat, when the assistant stage manager, Olga Bennett saw what she imagined to be a stagehand standing behind the wheelchair. The sight was so inconceivable that she could only imagine he was drunk and although at that point out of sight of the audience, was about to do something foolish, so she was considering bringing down the curtain when he simply vanished! When she had recovered her composure, she realised that the 'stagehand' had been wearing a frock coat, and when she described him it was clear she had seen Buckstone. Neither performer had been aware of the incident, but both subsequently testified to the reliability of Ms Bennett.

Donald Sinden CBE made his West End debut in 1949 at the Haymarket in a production of The Heiress, starring the late Ralph Richardson and Peggy Ashcroft. His part entailed all of seven lines, but as any young actor appreciates, the less the involvement the greater the build-up of apprehension, and to add to the trauma of a West End opening, the director who had been responsible for getting him the part left after a 'difference' with management three weeks into rehearsals – to be replaced by another director (John Gielgud), who proceeded to change everything.

Despite these trials and tribulations, the play was a great success, but Mr Sinden has another reason for remembering the run almost forty years later – because he was another who saw Buckstone's ghost. The incident happened when he and his stage fiancee, played by Gillian Howell were on their way from their dressing rooms at the top of the building down to the stage (there were so many stairs they had to set off several minutes before required to ensure they were not late for their entrance!). He recalls what happened in his autobiography, A Touch of The Memoirs

64

(Hodder & Stoughton 1982), from which he has allowed me to quote:

'Between 1853 and 1878 the Haymarket was under the successful management of J. B. Buckstone and his ghost is supposed to haunt the theatre. Supposed? No it *does* – I have seen it! One evening Gillian Howell and I received our call and as usual we started to walk down the stairs together. As we rounded the corner on to the landing outside Ralph's dressing room, we saw Ralph dressed in his costume of the 1860 period, deep in thought with his back to us, looking out of the window. We both said, "Good Evening". The fact that we received no reply did not worry us: we were used to Ralph's idiosyncratic individuality. We passed within two feet of him and continued on our way still gossiping. A flight and a half down we both stopped in our tracks and clutched each other. Ralph at that moment was on the stage in the middle of his first scene! I raced back up the stairs, but the figure had gone. There was no other member of the cast who could have been there – let alone in the period costume . . .'

Although he spent nearly ten successful years at the Haymarket, Beerbohm Tree (1853–1917) is associated more with Her Majesty's, which was built especially for him in 1897 – the fourth playhouse on that site – which he was to call 'my beautiful theatre'. Beerbohm Tree, a half brother of Max Beerbohm, became a professional actor at the age of twenty-five and rose to the top of his profession as, following fashion, he combined this with management. He had for some time wanted his own playhouse, and finally the success of *Trilby* across the road provided the finances to fulfil that dream. He must have had a flair for producing because his very first production – an adaptation of *The Seats of the Mighty* – ran for fourteen months. He consolidated his position with revivals of earlier successes, such as *Trilby*, and then mounted a succession of plays by Shakespeare in repertory, which were immediately the talk of the town. Beerbohm Tree was a creative artist who needed fresh challenges and became bored with long runs; he is on record as having described his version of *Henry VIII* as 'an obstinate success'. He was knighted by Edward VII in 1909.

Ask the regular staff at any theatre when the ghost walks

and the chances are that the answer will be – on a Friday, ie pay night (unless that happens to be on a Thursday!). The adage obviously refers to a hypothetical ghost, but Robert Stanton, mentioned before, is able to offer a different explanation from experience. When he was company manager of the production of *Teahouse of the August Moon* which played at Her Majesty's in the mid-1950s, one of his duties was to pay the wages. The wardrobe department was housed at the top of the building in what had once been Beerbohm Tree's flat.

Bob was talking to the wardrobe mistress, Margaret Hamilton, when she said, 'Don't look now, but Sir Beerbohm is just behind you.' He remembers that Margaret was psychic and claimed she saw the ghost of the great actor-manager quite often. In fact, only a few people have actually seen the figure of Beerbohm Tree, although dozens have felt a presence and the accompanying drop in temperature. However, in the 1970s practically the whole cast of Terence Rattigan's *Cause Célèbre* including its star, the late Glynis Johns, saw his shadowy but recognisable figure walking across the back of the stalls. According to the present-day housekeeper, Tom Mitchell, he seems to adhere to the routine followed during his lifetime – down side stairs from his flat to the back of the dress circle, then behind the back row of seats to another flight of stairs down.

His favourite seat was in a top box (stage right) and a few years ago during a spell in which Indian films were shown on Sundays, a couple complained to the manager that their enjoyment of the film was interrupted when the door suddenly opened and it became extremely cold in the box. Not having heard of the resident ghost their complaint was simply about doors which opened by themselves and the freezing draughts.

The Garrick in Charing Cross Road, near Trafalgar Square, has no connection with the great David Garrick, but it claims two very distinguished actor-managers of its own. They were John Hare, for whom the theatre was built by W. S. Gilbert in 1889 (and who was subsequently knighted for his services to theatre), and Arthur Bourchier, whose professional reputation is now somewhat eclipsed by his notoriety as the ghost which still haunts the theatre.

Hare, another outstanding actor now forgotten, starred

in a number of memorable plays, but the production which caused a sensation was *The Notorious Mrs Ebbsmith*, in which he played opposite Mrs Patrick Campbell. As with Pinero's trend-setting *The Second Mrs Tanqueray*, the subject matter broke new ground in the theatre and the excitement was heightened after a real-life Mrs Ebbsmith was found drowned in the Thames with a ticket for the play in her clothing; she had written to a friend that the play had preyed on her mind!

Bourchier who had begun his professional acting career in Lily Langtry's company, took over the Garrick licence in 1900, and embarked on an ambitious programme ranging from Shakespeare (in which he often starred with his actress wife, Violet Vanbrugh) to farce. He left in 1906 to concentrate on acting, and died in 1927 while on tour in South Africa. For this reason there was no immediate link between the early reports of supernatural happenings and the former actor-manager, since it seemed unlikely that he would bother to return from South Africa! Indeed, for some time if there was a ghost, it was somewhat fancifully identified as David Garrick, and it was not until the discovery of an old postcard showing Bourchier and his wife, that finally was the true ghost 'recognised'.

In the interim years it would have been possible to compile a dossier on the variety of strange happenings. A stage carpenter claimed to see the curtains rise and fall several times of their own accord. In 1940 during a run of *Meet Mr Callaghan*, one of the actors saw a man sitting in a chair in one of the upstairs rooms. Not recognising the stranger, he was about to speak to him when the apparition disappeared. Knocking noises so clear that they could not have been attributed to natural sounds, were such a regular feature that staff no longer reacted to them. At one stage there was a persistent spell of knocking on the box office door. When the staff inside grew tired of opening the door to find no one there, they would automatically call out 'Come in, David.'

However, none of these unsubstantiated reports could be accepted as evidence if it were not for Freddie Booth, linkman at the Garrick for the past thirty years, who has had so many strange experiences there, it is possible he may be psychic. When I met Mr Booth, the feature of his personality that impressed me most was his matter-of-fact acceptance of the presence of a benign, resident ghost – in the manner of a person who has no need to dramatise or embellish his anecdotes. He had only been in the job a short while when he had his first encounter with the paranormal. Standing by the stage door, he was talking to the house manager when the nearby glass swing doors were blown open by what he describes now as a 'gale' – a wind rushing up from the basement for no earthly reason. He was startled and asked for an explanation – to be told complacently that it was the ghost of David Garrick.

Within weeks he was to experience the first of many taps on the shoulder, although on one occasion in the dress circle he received a thump on the back which was sharp enough to send him staggering. The incident was witnessed by a long-serving usherette who guessed what had caused his stumble, because something similar had happened to her, although she had said nothing at the time in case management considered she was becoming eccentric. 'Yet I have never had any occasion to feel scared, or even uneasy,' Freddie told me. 'Even the thump, which was quite violent, seemed to have been done affectionately; it didn't really hurt – just caught me off balance.' Others have also been tapped on the shoulder, possibly indicating a sense of humour because Freddie remembers one usherette who had decided to take a doze between performances, and who fled in terror after being awakened by a hand on her shoulder. 'Every indication is that the ghost is that of someone who loves the theatre,' he maintains. 'The only time I've seen anything remotely destructive in what used to be a circle bar – when I saw a bottle rise off the shelf, perform a gentle arc and then smash on the ground, in the manner of a conjuring trick that went wrong.'

Freddie Booth is the only person I have traced who has actually seen what may have been the ghost of Arthur Bourchier. It happened one night when he was leaving the managing director's office on the first floor, and entering what is known as the 'phantom staircase' (although there is no significance in the name) which leads to the roof. It is a narrow, winding staircase similar to so many in larger theatres, and half way up is a door on the right which leads to the flies. In the doorway he encountered a man in the shadows; he was wearing a long cloak and a tall, wide-brimmed hat. 'He was standing right in front of me,' Freddie recalls, 'although unfortunately he was looking down as though deep in thought, so I couldn't see his face. I was obviously shaken because I didn't expect to find anybody up there, and his clothes were so very different, but by the time I had shaken my head he was gone.' He discovered later that Bourchier's old dressing room was now the managing director's office, and that he had used the phantom staircase all the time.

One of the more bizarre incidents which lasted for several days was during a run in 1980 of the play, *Death Trap*. Early in the play a mystery voice persisted not only in prompting the actors on stage, but actually speaking their lines a split second ahead of them. The obvious assumption was that a practical joker in the audience was responsible, even though it would have needed a clever ventriloquist to cope with a stage whisper. But when it happened with the next performance and it was appreciated that it was an almost impossible task to memorise *everyone's* lines, the stage management team conducted a thorough investigation. The voice was definitely coming from what had been the old prompt corner, but there was no one in sight, and it could not have been a tape recorder because the voice reacted to the actors, always jumping in a split second or so before – whether they were on cue or deliberately late. It stopped after several performances and no one was ever able to provide an explanation for the phenomenon.

There are so many truly beautiful playhouses dotted about the country, trying to compare them is meaningless; beauty lies in the eye of the beholder and we all have different views on the respective appeals of Georgian, Victorian, Edwardian and even very modern structures. However, a large number of people in the profession who play so many venues, as well as theatre-lovers able to travel, regard the Theatre Royal, Bath, as their favourite.

Built in 1805, third in the city's history, the Theatre Royal has at least one resident ghost, although I have passed on what is in many ways a more intriguing story – which may or may not have an element of the supernatural (see Chapter 10). The first playhouse was erected exactly one hundred years before on the site of what became better known as the Royal Mineral Water Hospital. It is believed that the city

Theatre Royal, Bath

had a transient theatre tradition, and the playhouse was designed to meet the requirements of the growing number of people moving to the area to 'take the waters'. The second in Orchard Street which opened in 1750 still stands, although when it was replaced by the present larger and more decorative building, it became a place of worship and subsequently a Masonic Hall. In 1768 the theatre was granted the royal patent and by the end of that century it was recognised as the country's most important playhouse outside London. Sarah Siddons first made her mark at Bath during the four years spent with what was then a permanent repertory company.

The new theatre got off to an impressive start and for the next twenty or so years more than maintained its promise. However, then its fortunes declined, culminating with a fire on Good Friday 1862 which virtually destroyed the building. Once it had been decided to rebuild on the existing site, rather than move, an architectural competition was held, and the winner was a local designer, C. J. Phipps, who went on to become the leading theatre designer of the later Victorian period (among his outstanding work was the Grand, Wolverhampton). Phipps's decorative scheme was mid-Victorian, including metal flowers around the cast-iron pillars supporting the balustrades), but the layout remained basically

Georgian. Redecorated in 1892 and 1974, with a major renovation in 1984, it looks much the same today.

Despite the number of distinguished actors and actresses
who have appeared here over the years, the theatre ghost is
believed to be that of a now forgotten actress of the early
nineteenth century who committed suicide in the Garrick Head
public house next door to the playhouse. Presumably she was
an attractive young woman, because legend has it that she
captivated a theatregoer who became a regular, sitting in
the same box, upper stage right, to watch her performance.
Inevitably, her husband became aware of a potential rival
and challenged the man to a duel – in which the customer was
killed. The present Theatre Royal management have nothing
in the archives to identify the actress, or to indicate what
actually happened, but it is assumed that the trauma was
too much for her – that after her final performance, she
went next door where she was staying – still wearing her
long grey dress and feathers in her hair – and hanged herself. There is another theory that she threw herself from a
window of the theatre.

It may not come as a surprise that some of the more spectacular tales of the Grey Lady come from the public house, once
a gambling den run by Beau Nash, and in recent years one of
the licensees had tee-shirts overprinted with an invitation to
come and meet their ghost. However, actual sightings in the
theatre have been infrequent. The Russian ballerina, Anna
Pavlova, did not know the legend when she danced here in
1920, but after one performance enquired about the woman
in feathers and a grey dress sitting in one of the boxes. No
one was able to help, and front of house staff insisted that
the box was unoccupied. Thirty years later, the late Anna
Neagle announced that she was aware of her presence; those
who knew Dame Anna would know that she was not given to
flights of fancy – indeed, she had starred in other shows in
which colleagues and stage management had claimed to experience one or other element of the supernatural, but which
had apparently escaped her attention.

The Royalty Theatre in Kingsway has been open for its
original purpose so infrequently that few Londoners are
aware of its existence. Whether this is due to a reputation of

being an unlucky theatre, or merely its slightly inaccessible position is impossible to tell.

Known for most of its life as the Stoll Theatre, it was for many years referred to as 'Hammerstein's Folly', being built in 1911 as the London Opera House by Oscar Hammerstein I, allegedly as a showcase for his mistress. It was not a success, quickly dropping down-market to stage reviews and panto-mimes, being 'dark' for several months in the year, until he sold it in 1916. The building was eventually acquired by Sir Oswald Stoll who turned it into a cinema, and for many years – according to George Hoare, Drury Lane archivist, who used to work for Stoll – the ghost of Hammerstein's protégé was reported at the back of the gallery; she was identified by a black lace mantilla worn earlier in one of her stage roles. Security men knew when she was around because their guard dogs would refuse to go near the gallery, displaying all the symptoms of fear we have come to expect when animals are faced with the supernatural. During World War II it became a theatre again, but fortunes were still at a low ebb and it closed again in 1957, after which the building was used for various other purposes, including a TV studio for many years. It reopened as a theatre in 1987.

5

LATER GENERATIONS

Theatre is very conscious of tradition. Books have been written about the great playhouses, although few have such grand origins; indeed, many have very modest histories. But as far as I know, there is only one professional theatre in the world which was born in a cow shed – the Byre Theatre, St Andrews. With standards as high as might be found anywhere in the British Isles, the Byre offers everything the theatregoer could want – including a resident ghost.

In 1933, a group of enthusiastic amateurs headed by the writer A. B. Paterson (who was to be awarded the MBE for services to theatre), ambitiously took a lease on the disused Old Byre of the Abbey Street Dairy Farm, owned by the town council. In his *History* of the St Andrews theatre, Mr Paterson writes about their first sight of the Byre, which had been used for some time as a potato merchant's store. 'Peering through the cobwebbed windows, I saw a rectangular chamber with the remains of cow stalls, partly removed to make way for potatoes. Above was a loft, where fodder had been stored for the cows. "This would be the very place for us," I announced.' A stage was built at one end, linked by a perpendicular ladder to the dressing rooms in the loft.

The new theatre was beginning to build a reputation when the outbreak of war deprived the company of its entire male membership. However, this setback coincided with the arrival of the man whose professional skills transformed the operation – Charles Marford, formerly stage director of the Old Vic, who as actor, stage director, scenic artist and producer, had worked with some of the great names of the theatre, notably Lilian Baylis for many years. Marford ran the company during the war period, putting on Shakespeare and short-cast plays, until he retired to Devon, where he died a few years later. But even retirement did not keep him away, returning in subsequent summers to produce, advise and act. It is his ghost which is supposed to haunt the theatre, even after 1970 when the Old Byre was pulled down and replaced by a purpose-built small theatre about forty yards from the original site.

Initially the reports were mainly from stage management, working through the night on the change-over of plays, and were usually of ghostly footsteps (which some claimed to identify as the distinctive tread of Charles Marford) in the dressing rooms. In 1959, the author Ian Curteis was directing a play at the Byre. 'One night after the show I had to go back for a script I'd left at the theatre,' he said later. 'The place was deserted but as I went through the stage door I heard heavy footsteps. I had been told the theatre was haunted by Charlie Marford, and in my panic I called out as loud as I could – "All right Charlie, if you're up there, stop that noise and come down!" The clumping footsteps stopped instantly. Then there was silence. Eventually I plucked up courage, and had a look round. Nobody!'

Perhaps the most intriguing incident was in the new theatre when the company was working on a change-over late on a Saturday night. Suddenly the familiar mix of scenery and lighting changes was punctuated by the record/tape player which started to play one of Charles Marford's favourite pieces of music. Nan Eagle, the caretaker, who is still with the company, remembers those startling few seconds vividly – although she cannot recall the title of the music.

The backstage team stopped, transfixed, and when it ended Andrew Cowie, the stage manager went over to the player to investigate. On it he found, not the tape they had heard – but the one that had originally been set-up for the interval earlier – a totally different piece. Yet years later Nan remains convinced that what they all heard was Marford's favourite – however it was relayed!

One of the new generation of theatres, the Leicester Haymarket (it only opened in 1973), already has a reputation for the ambitious scale of its productions and for artistic excellence. Despite its short history, much the same can be said for the wealth of paranormal activity – which is likely to have something to do with what was originally on the site.

In addition to fairly common phenomena (eg Albert Asher, the night watchman, was once driven to distraction by lights coming on again in the production area minutes after he had switched them off – despite the fact that he would often *wait* to make certain), there have been a number of sightings. One ghost – that of a child dressed in an Edwardian sailor suit – was seen in close-up by former company manager, Soozie Copley, whose experience is unique in my experience because of the secondary 'physical' evidence of its presence.

The incident took place in 1975 when *The Caucasian Chalk Circle* was running in repertoire with *Joseph and his Technicolour Dreamcoat* which, between them, had an unusually large cast of children. Soozie, now a lecturer at the Guildhall School of Music and Drama, believes it may have been their presence that attracted the boy in the sailor suit. 'The Brecht play had already opened and although it only involved a couple of child actors, I always felt there were psychic overtones in the scene where the women struggle for possession of the child in the circle,' she said. 'We were very busy with rehearsals for the production and I was working well into the night on props and various odds and ends. Apart from one of the electricians, I was alone at about 3 in the morning when I saw a child of about six or seven, dressed in a sailor suit.

'What I saw was so real, so bright and colourful that for a moment or two I imagined he was a child actor from one of the shows. He was struggling to turn the handle of the pass-door to the stage, and I called out to ask where he thought he was going. It was only when he vanished that I realised what time it was, and that his clothes were so different from anything we had in wardrobe. Even so, he seemed real enough for me to want to see if he had actually opened the door and gone through – but I forgot about that when I tried the handle and found it *wet*.' Assuming it was not condensation on the handle – and Soozie assures me it was not, it is the first case I have encountered of a spirit leaving visible and tactile traces of its appearance. There is no clue to the identity of the sailor boy, although Ms Copley did make some enquiries later. 'I discovered that in the nineteenth century there were some houses backing on to the site on which the theatre was built, and a well in which a child was supposed

75

to have been drowned. But it is impossible to speculate on whether it was the same boy.'

During that spell, Margaret Walton, then box office manager, was working late with a colleague when they saw the door from the auditorium to the foyer open slightly, and a small hand appear. 'The public had long since gone,' she remembers, 'and from the size of the hand we jumped to the conclusion it belonged to a child who had been left behind, or one of the actors. The door is very heavy and it opened just a crack – enough for us to see the hand – and then closed again. We went to look, imagining the door was too heavy for a child, but when we looked there was no one inside.' In fact there have been a number of sightings of the 'complete' sailor boy – the most public being in 1981 during a production of *Hamlet*. As Ophelia's funeral bier was lowered through the stage, Ophelia (played by Mavis Blake) saw the boy waiting for her although he disappeared almost immediately.

Soozie Copley also recalls another strange incident during a production of *Blithe Spirit*. During a play when the team might have expected some supernatural manifestation nothing untoward happened except towards the end of the rehearsal period. 'One of the props was a piano which had an electric motor to make it play of its own accord at the end. We were having notes after the run-through, and I asked someone to switch off the motor and give me the key so it didn't get mislaid. We had practically finished notes when the piano suddenly came to life and started playing. Obviously it came as a surprise, but then we had got used to that sort of thing at the Haymarket.' (See also Chapter 10.)

6

VARIETY HOUSES

Although variety had gained a particularly strong hold in the North, the long battle with television was doomed to failure. Of well over a hundred theatres in the North East alone (part of a boom which followed the great railways expansion of the nineteenth century), the Darlington Hippodrome, now known as the Civic, is one of only four that remain. Built as a music hall in 1907, the Hippodrome won its reputation on the entrepreneurial skills of its first proprietor, Rino Pepi, a born showman, who already had a successful career as a quick-change artiste. Pepi's first programme included not only top variety acts, but what was billed as the Pepiscope, his own bioscope of moving pictures, featuring the latest news. Signor Pepi was very much a local institution by the time he died in November 1927.

In 1966, the town council took over responsibility for the theatre, which then officially became known as the Civic, and when it was renovated, workmen came across a small grave containing the bones of Signor Pepi's Pekinese dog. Front of house staff claimed they had often heard mysterious whining sounds around the circle staircase, and there was also talk of a shadowy figure standing in the centre stalls. But although there have been strange incidents it has not been possible to identify the ghostly forms. Indeed, the story is probably based on the knowledge that Signor Pepi wanted to be buried next to his wife, Countess Rossetti, at Barrow-in-Furness, but en route a storm blew up and his body had to be kept overnight at a roadside inn – a delay which gave his spirit the opportunity to return to his beloved theatre, and his dog!

Nevertheless it does seem that one of the resident ghosts is someone interested in the theatre, and there have been a number of sightings in what is now a coffee bar. Marketing executive, Stephen Luck, had an unusual experience in 1987 when he was using the room, empty at lunchtime, to spread out a selection

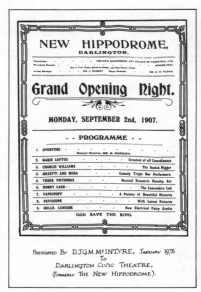

New Hippodrome, Darlington: (left) the original silk programme of the 1907 opening and (right) Signor Pepi's box

of posters on the tops of coffee tables. Bending over, he became conscious of someone behind him. Without moving he looked under his arm and saw a pair of black shoes and dark trousers – which was the range of his vision from that position. Assuming that it was theatre director, Brian Goddard, he sought the newcomer's advice on the posters: 'Do you think these are better than . . .' He turned round for a reaction, but there was no one. 'If it had been Brian, or one of the staff, there was no way they could have left the room so quickly,' he points out.

In their belief that the spirit that keeps a benevolent eye on them is that of Signor Pepi, the staff are not alarmed by such experiences, but something more unpleasant happened in 1955 when Ray Mancell, manager of Her Majesty's in London, but then a young singer, appeared at the Hippodrome as a featured vocalist in a variety show. Because the chorus girls had a number of changes, he swapped dressing rooms and took their room at the top of the building. On the first night he was applying his make-up when it suddenly became icy cold, and he was conscious of someone crossing the room behind him. He looked round, and although there was no one there, out of the corner of his eye he glimpsed a shadow go straight through a partition

78

wall. 'It was a very unpleasant experience,' he recalls, 'but I'd never been to the theatre before, so I tried to kid myself I had imagined it all. Later, when I told someone about it and where it happened, I learned that some years before a flyman had been found hanging upside down from one of the ropes, after an argument with his wife or girl friend. In a later conversion, part of the flies was partitioned-off, and a dressing room put in. That was where the ghost walked.'

Other less sinister sightings include a ballerina and a stage manager. In the mid-1960s, one of the early morning cleaners saw a young ballerina dancing on stage. On leaving the auditorium she asked the supervisor the girl's identity. Told that it was not possible because none of the artistes had arrived, they went back to check, only seconds later – but the dancer had vanished. Almost twenty years later, a member of the 'Second Generation' dance group left some companions in the circle bar to fetch a holdall from his dressing room. Returning a few minutes later, he enquired the way out of the building – but having been given instructions, he appeared surprised. 'Oh, but that was the way I've just been,' he retorted. 'I saw someone locking up.' When the theatre staff seemed puzzled, he explained: 'On the stairs I bumped into an elderly man locking and chaining up the dressing rooms. He was heading for the exit.' He was then informed that there was no elderly member of the staff, but when he described the man, someone remembered a former stage manager who had died some years before. The description fitted him in every respect!

In 1987, Stephen Luck was duty manager one night during a run of *Seven Brides for Seven Brothers*, which meant that as last to leave, he had to lock up. In due course, the stage manager reported that he had already turned off all the lights and locked every door – except dressing room one, used by several of the chorus, because one of the dancers was still changing. Eventually, Stephen was able to switch off the remaining light and close up. He left the theatre in total darkness and popped over to the pub across the road. Forty minutes later, the publican casually asked what was 'going on' across the road. Stephen shook his head, pointing out that he had just locked up, whereupon the publican drew the curtains aside to reveal the theatre – in a blaze of light.

79

Although the bright lights made it unlikely, burglars seemed the only logical alternative, so Stephen asked if someone would accompany him while he went back to check. Unlocking the stage door, they found no sign of intruders – but all the lights were on. On the main electricity control board, *every* switch had been turned on – illuminating not only outside, but auditorium, backstage and offices, as well as the heating which had not been in use. 'I know it wasn't anyone from the theatre playing a joke,' Stephen insisted. 'They care too much about the place to waste money on that scale. If I hadn't been so near, the electricity would have been on all night!'

Speaking of legacies of the past, Newcastle's Tyne Theatre & Opera House, which opened in 1867, is still much admired for the powerful assembly of Victorian backstage machinery which over the years enabled it to mount Hollywood-style spectacles. But in 1887, a 36lb cannonball, one of eight used in a thunder-roll machine, broke through a safety net and killed a stage carpenter – prompting a legend that his ghost now haunts the theatre. But I fear the recently restored wooden equipment backstage is much more impressive than the ghost legend which is unsupported by any worthwhile evidence.

One of the province's most famous theatres, the Palace, Manchester, opened in 1891 with the idea of bringing 'culture' to the North – but within three years, after some financially disastrous highbrow programmes, it set out successfully on the road to become the home of variety – attracting all the greatest stars. Its reputation for professional excellence has been maintained to this day despite economic setbacks in the 1970s which resulted in the Palace, and its rival theatre the Opera House, being taken over by the civil engineering and construction company, Norwest Holst.

The Palace's Grey Lady, reputed to be that of a cleaner who died on the premises, has been seen on a number of occasions, sometimes clearly, at others as a grey haze. The former sightings include that by a workman engaged in major renovations before the theatre reopened in 1981, when he used one of the ladies' toilets (the 'new' men's room was not yet ready). However, the cubicle partitions were not in place and he was disconcerted to see an elderly woman sitting in a corner, looking at him. He averted his eyes, and when he looked again she was sitting in another corner. When she vanished he did not know whether to be scared, or relieved! Another, in 1987, was when 'Geordie', a member of the house staff, decided to take a shower. He was about to enter dressing room 14 when, through the glass panelled fire-door he saw a woman cleaner going into dressing room 15 at the end of the corridor. Deciding to warn her of his intentions he followed her – but there was no one in dressing room 15 – which had no other exit.

Laurence McBride, one of the stage door staff, has to complete his nightly duties with a security check of the building. In 1985, having started at the top he finished in the stalls by the orchestra pit. As a final 'gesture' he shone his torch into the grand tier (upper circle) and stopped at what appeared to be a patch of grey smoke. His automatic reaction was that someone had disobeyed the no-smoking rule in the auditorium and left one burning. Clearly noting the position, he hurried to investigate – but there was nothing to be found. Two years later, something similar happened when he finished his rounds and actually killed the emergency lights so that the place was in total darkness. 'I was standing by the orchestra pit rail and for no particular reason glanced up at the circle,' he recalls. 'I saw a pinhead of light – it might have been the size of a fairy light but from that distance seemed smaller. My first thought was that it was coming from outside until I remembered that the doors at the back of the circle were closed. Then there was another light in another part, and then another, until it looked like a myriad display. It was a very weird experience.'

There is so much real-life drama in the history of the Theatre Royal, Glasgow – the first two theatres were destroyed by fire (1879 and 1895), and at least two people have died in tragic circumstances – that one would be surprised not to encounter a troubled spirit. Moreover, like most playhouses with a proud tradition, the Theatre Royal, owned by Scottish Opera since 1974, would love to show off a ghost of its own. Indeed, they do lay claim to a couple – although somewhat half-heartedly – and evidence is in such short supply that I have only included the theatre in the hope that more psychic readers pay them a visit and turn something up.

Rumour has it that the first of these theatres was haunted by a former manager's dog which appeared lifelike but would completely ignore everyone, and food and sweetmeats offered by friendly theatre personnel. Any element of the supernatural connected with the present building, designed by the great C. J. Phipps in 1895, would presumably be that of a female ghost, Norah, or of a fireman who was drowned in the sub-basement below the stage in the 1960s when the place was owned by Scottish TV.

According to theatre manager, David Jackson, 'Norah' has never been identified, and is thought to be either a woman cleaner with a special fondness for the place, or a jilted young woman who threw herself over the balcony – although he can find no record of this event. 'She has been "felt" in the second circle and some of the cleaners maintain she inhabits dressing room S4, which is connected with the circle by a pass-door,' he told me. 'The only suggestion of a spirit in the sub-basement came from a contractor's electrician working alone down there after the reopening in 1975 when he heard his name being called. I was up in the third circle at the time, and he came up a hundred stairs at the double in a state of shock, but I didn't know him well enough to judge whether or not he was a reliable witness. Unfortunately, there has been no proper corroboration in either case.'

The Birmingham Alexandra opened as the Lyceum in 1901 to such dismal attendances that within a year it had been sold for little more than £4,000 – less than half the cost it took to build! The new owner who renamed it in honour of Queen Alexandra, was a flamboyant showman of the old school, Lester Collingwood (he had already made his mark as a moustache-twirling villain in his own touring shows), and his first decision was to introduce melodrama and pantomime which were to prove an immediate success. Eight years later he was driving to Sheffield for an assignation with an actress (women being his main interest outside the Alex), and was killed in a collision with a milk float; this afforded him the dubious honour of being one of the first in Britain to be killed in a road accident. He had become so identified with the Alex and its now established reputation, that at his funeral the streets were lined with mourners.

It is a measure of the accomplishments of Leon Salberg, the man who succeeded him a year later (1911), that it is his ghost rather than that of Lester Collingwood, which purportedly haunts the theatre. Indeed, every supernatural incident over the years has been attributed to Leon – until a degree of confusion was introduced in 1987 when a cleaner saw the ghost of a *woman* who has not been identified. Certainly Mr Salberg made an enormous contribution to the development of the Alex, which included a major rebuilding programme in 1935, after which he was succeeded by his son Derek who, at twenty-four, was Britain's youngest theatre director. Leon died at the theatre in 1938, which is why it is assumed he is still 'tied' to the building.

At the end of the 1960s the theatre was acquired by the Birmingham Corporation, which leased it back to a company headed by Derek Salberg, and the availability of fresh funds meant that in 1968 a modern extension, stretching across the road (via a closed-in connecting bridge), placed the Alex's new frontage in a more prominent position. When Derek retired in 1977 he was awarded the OBE, subsequently upgraded to CBE.

Mr Tony Pugh, who was manager and licensee for ten years until 1987, remains convinced of the presence of a benevolent spirit, although he accepts the suggestion that it was a convenient habit that made him and others assume it was the ghost of Leon Salberg. 'Apart from the many specific incidents, for much of the time I was conscious of a presence,' he told me, 'particularly in the offices upstairs, which were used as rehearsal rooms when we were a repertory company. I spent a considerable amount of time alone there in the evenings, and there was quite a lot of psychic activity – such as doors opening and closing without cause. Yet it never bothered me; in fact, it was quite a nice feeling, as though I was among friends.'

Mr Pugh had so many strange experiences that I have restricted my account to events when there was a witness to corroborate his evidence. The only sighting was one evening in 1982 when he was in the Leon bar – the room once used as Leon Salberg's office – talking to the barman, Derek Evans. There are two entrances – one for the public from the auditorium, and the other from backstage. 'For some unaccountable reason we both happened to look at the public door just at the moment when a very positive shadow came through,' he recalls. 'I couldn't be sure if it was a man or woman, but the outline was in a human form, and clear enough to grab our attention.

The shadow was apparently unaware of us and went straight past, through what used to be a doorway – now covered in – to backstage, and Leon's private box upstairs. It was too much for Derek who left in a hurry.'

On a Saturday night in 1985 after the performance and the public and staff had gone, Mr Pugh was standing by the closed Bridge Bar (situated in the bridge which straddles the road) talking to the doorman, Raymond Savage. The building was locked and in darkness, although the bar area had the benefit of the street lights outside. From the direction of the foyer they heard the approaching sound of keys jingling. 'It was obviously a bunch of keys,' Tony maintains. 'I knew the sound because my own theatre keys made a similar noise. We knew there was no one in the building, yet the sound was distinct enough to make us stop talking and concentrate on whoever was approaching. We could see quite well from the street lights and soon it was obvious that there was no one there, although the sound was coming nearer. Eventually it went past, as though someone jingling keys had gone by within two or three feet of us. We knew instinctively this was a paranormal experience, but trying to cling to reality and knowing that sound *can* carry and be distorted, we separated to search the surrounding area in case there was someone about – but, of course, we didn't find anyone.'

A few years earlier, the police had received a tip-off that the IRA were planning to bomb public places, so additional security staff were employed, mainly to search people entering the theatre. 'They were a pretty tough bunch, yet one was reduced to a trembling wreck one night when he was walking through the back of the stalls, and felt an invisible hand on his shoulder. I've never seen a man so terrified,' Tony recalls.

However, the latest incident in 1987 occurred shortly after a new firm of contract cleaners had been employed. One of the women cleaners arriving early in the morning, unlocked the only door to the small Garrick Bar and set to work. She was vacuuming the carpet when the motor suddenly cut out, prompting her to go over to the electric plug and 'fiddle' with it until it started again. However, the movement was shortlived and while she was trying to get the vacuum to work she glanced up and saw in the well of the bar a woman dressed completely in grey. 'She hadn't heard about our ghost,' Alan Galloway, the chief electrician assured me, 'so her only reaction was to wonder how anyone could have entered such a small room without being seen. As she stared, the figure just vanished. From her description we think it could have been the ghost of a former wardrobe mistress – which comes as a surprise because we believed that Leon was our only ghost.'

There are rumours of ghosts at the Grand Theatre, Wolverhampton – another of Charles J. Phipps's elegant designs, and one of the finest Victorian theatres in the Midlands – but the 1980s was a period of transition and I was unable to find anyone who could speak from first hand experience. The theatre, opened in December 1894, had done very well for many years but hit a bad patch in the 1970s which culminated in closure, before reopening three years later after a £1 million restoration programme. With the departure of most of the long-serving members of staff disappeared proper evidence of the stories I had heard. In fact, the only person who had an even indirect connection was Tom Latham who had been house manager for forty-three years (his father having been stage manager for thirty-five years!), who recalled that several people believed the ghost to have been that of another former manager, Percy Purdey, who had continued to occupy a flat in the theatre even after his retirement, and who died after World War II.

Mr Purdey had a reputation for being a man of habit; to quote Mr Latham, 'You could tell the time by his routine. Every night when the curtain had gone up, he would without fail pop into the bar for a whisky. For a time in the 1950s two of our women staff were convinced they could hear his footsteps. They would be at the bar preparing ices and soft drinks for the interval when they both heard footsteps coming down from the upstairs flat and approach the bar – but when they looked there was no sign of anyone.' Indicating that he did not believe in ghosts, Mr Latham added: 'They were very sensible women – I worked with one of them for many years – so I couldn't discount what they thought they saw – especially as it wasn't an isolated incident.'

7

SPIRITS INHERITED

In circumstances where there is no background of drama, ghosts can be associated with the site itself. The impressive Eden Court Theatre, on the banks of the River Ness, in Inverness, seems to have attracted two ghosts from its ostensibly tranquil setting – one from the old Bishop's Palace which it incorporates; the other from the Palace gardens in which it stands.

The 'new' (1976) multi-faceted arts complex, consists of an 810 seat auditorium, 70 seat cinema, art gallery, restaurant and bars, as well as the usual offices. The most frequent 'visitor', known as the 'Green Lady', is reputedly the ghost of Bishop Eden's wife who is supposed to have hanged herself in the palace's chapel, now the theatre's Green Room. The ghost of a child spotted in the lower levels of the theatre, is supposed to have been that of someone buried in the garden, although there are no records to support this theory. It seems feasible that the ground might at one stage have been consecrated, but research into the history of the Palace has been somewhat frustrating. All that is factually known is that the Palace was completed in 1878, as a golden wedding gift from the Diocese, but it was the Bishop and his wife who donated the six acres of land in which the house was set.

There is a surviving letter from Bishop Robert Eden to a fellow Bishop from a London address and written in June 1911, in which he raised the question of hauntings at Eden Court. '. . .When your brother was with me having come to preach, like a good Jacobite, in honour of King Charles the Martyr at Old St Pancras, he had a ghost story to tell me about Eden Court, to the effect that the garden there is "walked" by the ghost of a little girl, who appeared and disappeared to the terror of some of the poeple about the place. I should be greatly interested if you could kindly find time

86

to tell me what you can about it, and, among other things, whether the appearance is that of a poor child or of one of a higher social position. This story also reminds me of a rather weird thing which Bishop Kelly told me not very long after he went to live at Eden Court, and that is that the bell of the big bedroom used to ring at times of (apparently) its own accord, when there was no one in the room to ring it. Does this still go on?'

Unfortunately there is no evidence of a response to that enquiry, so we may never know.

One of the more recent sightings of the 'Green Lady' was in 1985 when projectionist and stagehand, Martin MacPhee, working all night, saw a ghostly figure on the upper landing of the staircase in the Bishop's Palace hallway. In fact, what he described was a 'dull green glow' which he assumed to be 'her' – without, in retrospect, being certain that it was a woman. Unfortunately, Martin lost his nerve and fled without waiting to check. In the following year, Graham Fraser, a stagehand, and James Farquhar, sound technician, were watching *Amadeus* in the circle of the complex cinema when they both became conscious of someone moving behind them. Since they were alone, and the circle was closed to the public they turned round to see who had joined them. They had not imagined it because they then saw a dark figure moving towards the back exit. Puzzled, they phoned down to the foyer usherette, and when she confirmed that the circle doors were locked, they told her nevertheless to expect someone coming down – but no one did appear.

I am indebted to Nick McClintock, the assistant house manager for checking the above experiences and for recording other unexplained incidents, such as the time during the January 1986 pantomime season when donkeys in the cast were found wandering in the grounds after being locked in for the night. Staff testified to having left the animals in their makeshift but secure stable, yet next morning the door was shut with the padlock still in place. Nobody has a clue as to how they got out. In 1987, one of the theatre administrators working alone late at night heard the photocopying machine in action. When she went in to investigate, the machine stopped, leaving a pile of paper as evidence of what it had been doing. Knowing that the machine had been switched off earlier, the witness – one of the few members of staff who does not believe in the resident ghost – remains mystified to this day.

The first playhouse on the site of the present Theatre Royal, York, was built in 1744 over the vaulted cloisters of the medieval St Leonard's Hospital (the remains of which can still be seen in places), served with supreme dedication by a small order of nuns. The Grey Lady, seen in different parts of the building over the years, is believed to have come from that hospital. Medieval orders endured the most barbaric practices in the name of religion, and there is some evidence that the famous Grey Lady may not be the only unfortunate spirit still 'time-bound'.

Initially, the theatre operated a touring company, but when a royal patent was obtained in 1869, the inevitable rise in status (coupled with the attraction of York Races) enabled it to attract the fashionable names of the London stage. However, success was sporadic, and the only consistent features were improvements incorporated through major renovations in the nineteenth century, and finally in 1967 when an imaginative modern glass front of house was set into the existing structure (if you will forgive a sweeping over-simplification); with the auditorium also getting a face-lift in 1978. The combination makes the Theatre Royal one of the most attractive repertory theatres in the country.

The problem with the Grey Lady in particular is that few

Eden Court Theatre, Inverness

eye-witnesses have come away with a clear picture. Yet ask most long-serving members of the staff for a description, and you will be assured that she wears a grey habit and white headdress; moreover that she was a novice who had disobeyed an instruction and that part of her punishment was that she must never leave the place, an order complicated by the fact that the Mother Superior died before the penance was lifted. Like so many legends which may have sprung up through wild speculation, the years have given the story credibility. But, in fact, the clearest sighting seems to have been during the major alterations in 1967 when one of the workmen saw a woman in grey he took to be the theatre housekeeper. But when she paid him no attention he told a member of the staff who pointed out there was no one around fitting that description – apart, he said, from the Grey Lady. The information did not amuse the workman who decided the location had suddenly become unhealthy, and it was time for him to move on!

However, since a ghost should not have a material form, we do not necessarily receive a realistic 'flesh and blood' image. Far less clear-cut, yet more impressive in other respects was an incident in August 1975 when the cast of *Dear Octopus* saw something which was certainly no natural phenomenon. It happened in final rehearsals, when the cast – few of whom, if any, knew the legend – were on stage, and the auditorium and backstage were empty apart from the director, Richard Digby Day (now artistic director of the Lyric Theatre, Belfast), and stage management team. The 'star', Evelyn Laye, had a solo item in the second act when she sat at the piano and, reminiscing, sang an extract from 'The Kerry Dances'. Thirteen years later the scene is imprinted on her memory. 'I was facing the auditorium, and suddenly at one end of the dress circle I became conscious of a small greyish-white mist,' she told me. 'Although it wasn't immediately identifiable, it had a human shape – and I thought it was a nun – but there wasn't time to study it properly because it began to drift across the circle. I'd carried on playing and when I finished the mist seemed to contract into a small ball, and disappeared.'

Whether Miss Laye actually imagined she was seeing a nun – or whether, because she takes an interest in spiritualism, she jumped to conclusions – it is impossible to say. The 'mist' moving across the dress circle was seen by everyone although most believe it had no particular shape, but then there was no rational explanation for its presence – there was no one in the circle and no one was smoking anywhere in the auditorium.

However, Richard Digby Day, has not for nothing earned his reputation as a thorough director. Although Miss Laye had been professional enough to soldier on, the distraction had spoilt the scene, and the director insisted they run through it again. When they got to the same song, the mist suddenly reappeared, and remained until the music stopped. This time Mr Digby Day announced that they had been visited by the Grey Lady, and a double appearance meant a successful show – which it was. Miss Laye was invited back ten years later to repeat her performance, but this time the Grey Lady – if that is who it was – did not put in an appearance.

Julie Dawn Cole is another actress to have seen what may have been the Grey Lady, although she could not identify her as a nun. The incident occurred in December 1976 when the cast of *Charlie's Aunt* were in the theatre's Green Room, rehearsing for an additional lunch-time show of seasonal Victorian entertainment. Julie was sitting apart from her colleagues. As they were running through different harmonies for a rendition of 'Jerusalem', Julie – still new to the theatre – was gazing at her surroundings as she sang. In turning her head she caught a glimpse of a figure standing in front of a wrought iron gate. Knowing that only a few of the actors were in the room to rehearse, she wondered for a moment if she had imagined the figure.

'I thought if I turned back slowly so that nobody would notice, it would have gone,' she told me. 'I did just that, holding my breath. But it was still there – a figure in a long cloak . . . I got the impression it was long, although I didn't see below the knee . . . with a hood. It was facing the other way and I couldn't see a face, but although the sex was not apparent, I knew instinctively it was a woman. The cloak was a shimmering white – not a deep colour, but rather like the glistening effect of petrol on a wet road. I was able to study her for more than a minute – it seemed ages – hoping she would turn round so I could see her features. She had actually started to turn when instead she vanished. I did not say anything to the others – it seemed so ridiculous. I'd never heard of the Grey Lady, so I was not thinking about ghosts, and I certainly wasn't scared; in fact, quite the reverse – she had quite a calming effect on me. But then about half an hour later I plucked up enough courage to suggest that I *might* have seen something untoward. Someone went to fetch Frank (the stage door keeper) who made me repeat the story. Frank said I had seen the Grey Lady and told me her story.'

Julie had a footnote about the following night, when they were back in the Green Room, sitting in a semi-circle as they rehearsed the same extracts. 'I felt something knock the back of my head – rather like when someone moves along the row behind you in the cinema – except that there was no one behind us. Then I noticed the girl next to me react in much the same way, and she suddenly commented on how cold it had become, and that she was "freezing". I reached out to touch her hand, and it was ice cold. Again, I knew intuitively that something supernatural had brushed past us, although I was not aware of any drop in temperature.'

In the early 1960s an exorcism to 'release' the troubled spirit of another nun was carried out by a professional singer who happened to be a clairvoyant and whose lengthy study of the occult qualified her to undertake such an ordeal. She is Murry Hope who has since become a writer on such subjects as parapsychology and ancient religions, but was then a member of the English Opera Company on tour in York.

Shortly after their arrival, one of the opera company's wardrobe staff, in charge of wigs, had a frightening experience when an apparition – she could only describe it as a 'dark shape' – appeared to emerge from one of the walls in her room, cross to the other side, and disappear through the far wall. Not happy about having to work alone in that room and knowing of Murry's interest in the occult, she asked if she could 'take it away'. Ms Hope had already worked for some years with a group that made a study of psychic phenomena and exorcism in particular, but had been trained to work in pairs, adhering to what was regarded as a 'safe' procedure. As there was no one of such experience on hand, she asked colleague, Gillian Ashby (who still sings with the ENO) if she would stay with her while she used her 'inner sense' to try to ascertain what was causing the presence. Her observations of what then transpired are fascinating. Here is what she described to me:

'It has been my experience that old buildings acted as recorders for highly emotionally charged events or sufferings that had taken place. Therefore one is likely to uncover not one but several dramatic overlays when probing a haunting of this kind. I found this to be the case at York, but since it was one particular phantasm I had been asked to remove, I concentrated on the description I had been given by the wardrobe assistant . . .' [The method Murry Hope employed would take too long to explain within the scope of this guide].

Contact having been made, what she now saw was a nun in black. 'I became aware of a woman who had been in Orders, who had suffered a severe emotional shock as a result of punishment meted out for some violation of the accepted moral codes of the time. This appeared to have involved solitary confinement, mental torture, and finally being walled up to die. I tried to make contact with that element of her consciousness that remained out of its correct time-zone, but although she acknowledged my approach she seemed too frightened to leave the precincts, indicating that no one could possibly release her.

'The type of religious mental programming issued in those days would tend to instil the psyche with a sense of "hell eternal", so it was difficult for me to break through such forceful conditioning. Finally, I told the entity to hold on to me, so that I could lead her out into the world beyond, where she would be free to see what the finger of history had written since the time of her demise. Previous experience had taught me that this usually worked, as the psyche-fragment in question could then become aware of the passage of time and the fact that it was no longer confined to the earthly conditions of its former time-zone. Having no one to help me, this proved to be something of a traumatic experience, as I found myself taking on the mental anguish and sufferings of the deceased. I made my way to the open door, but passing through it was the most difficult part of all as the "pull" on my aura was immense. But with much mental effort I made it, and with her I experienced the sense of amazement and wonder as the new view of the outside world slowly made its impact on her psyche-fragment. I was then aware of other "helpers" from her own dimension who came forward to assist her in the transition. Slowly the sense of weight fell from me and I was free of her. The whole experience, however, left me feeling shattered and exhausted. But this was because I had not worked correctly with a second trained person in the way I had been taught. I had done many exorcisms prior to this and subsequently carried out many, many more, but as this was the only incident where I worked "outside the rules", I never encountered the debilitating effect in any of the others.'

Having attended an exorcism in other circumstances, I must concede that because there is no audible response to the person conducting the ceremony, from the observer's perspective there is no immediate 'evidence' that his/her objective has been achieved. And while their sincerity is not in doubt, it is impossible to 'prove' that the clairvoyant is not deluding him or herself under the influence of self-hypnosis. However, if we understand what is taking place we must use our own judgement in deciding the validity of the exercise. My cautious instinct tells me that Murry Hope achieved what she set out to do, in private, and with no ulterior motive other than to help a troubled spirit. The sequence of events was, of course, witnessed by Gillian Ashby who says that although she was a passive onlooker, she tried to help in a small way by concentrating her thoughts on what her friend was trying to do. Whether or not it was successful, there have been no subsequent sightings of a Black Nun.

On the Grey Lady, Murry Hope adds: 'I never met her while I was at the theatre – one experience of that nature being enough to cope with in a week of intensive rehearsals and a heavy singing schedule. I was aware of her existence, but she did not seem to bother anyone during the period of our stay. Had a full psychic probe been made of the place, doubtless several emotionally disturbed entities would have put in an appearance. Such appalling things went on in these places, it is small wonder that the resulting traumas left their dark mark on the place of their enactment.'

In common with other university-financed theatres struggling to survive in the harsh climate for the arts in the late

1980s, the Oxford Playhouse was actually forced to close in 1987 in the depressing knowledge it would be at least a year before sufficient funds could be found to reopen on a viable basis. Hopefully, the Playhouse, built in 1938, will find a fresh impetus in its fiftieth anniversary year as it did thirty years ago when Frank Hauser arrived to save the day in not dissimilar circumstances.

Although fifty years is barely long enough to attract a resident ghost, the Playhouse claims a White Lady, presumably the ghost of a Carmelite nun from a medieval burial ground. When the builders were laying the foundations on land which had no record of burials, they discovered fifteen skulls subsequently dated to that period. There have been several sightings over the years – the last in 1978 when a staff cleaner, Mrs Frieda Dickens, who had previously had no time for ghost stories had reason to change her mind.

The incident took place in a basement room where Mrs Dickens was gathering together her mops and pails. 'The woman simply came out of the wall,' she recalled. 'I could see her quite clearly right in front of me – she had a thin face partly covered by a white veil. Then she drifted, or floated past me and disappeared through the brickwork at the opposite end. It was 8.30 in the morning and I was anxious to get on with the job, so I certainly wasn't daydreaming.'

Barry Sheppard, administrator until the theatre closed, is convinced that Mrs Dickens's account was genuine. 'We spoke to her very soon afterwards and there is no question she saw what she claimed,' he told me. 'Whether what she saw was a ghost in the traditional sense is another matter.'

While it might be assumed that the attractive White Rock Theatre, Hastings, opened in 1927 by the Prince of Wales (later Edward VIII, and Duke of Windsor) is a little short on history to have its own ghost, we must remember it was built on the site of a hospital incorporating its own mortuary. Coincidence or not, there may well be a supernatural presence which probably pre-dates the theatre, and although seen very rarely, it seems to have been active from time to time. Admittedly, those assumptions do not really measure up to the scientific criteria I have tried to attain, but it is reasonable to suppose that as all paranormal activity has occurred 'front of house' at the White Rock, the resident spirit has little interest in the building as a place of entertainment.

There was a cleaner who often complained of seeing 'something' moving when the building was supposed to be empty, but no one took her seriously. In fact, the only eye-witness I have been able to trace is Marion Hartley, who was in charge of the theatre bars until 1985, leaving with her husband, David, the theatre manager, to run their own pub in Kent. The incident occurred after the theatre had been extensively refurbished a year or so before. She had arrived early one morning – well before 8am – to clean out the pipes from the bar pumps to beer barrels.

'As I unlocked the doors to the bar lounge, I was immediately conscious of an elderly man sitting in a chair in the far corner,' she told me a couple of years later. 'There was only about fifteen feet between us so I could see him quite clearly. He was wearing a faded raincoat, and from the way he was positioned he appeared to be quite tall. The trouble is I jumped to conclusions because he reminded me of one of the cleaners – a man I knew as Charlie – so I didn't study his features. It wasn't until it suddenly dawned on me that Charlie couldn't have got in without the keys – which were in my possession – that I had any reason to doubt it was him. The alarm system was still activated, which means that it would have gone off – and stayed on. But when I turned to ask how he had got in, he had vanished. As I was in the doorway he couldn't have left the room.'

Marion admits that she often felt uneasy in certain parts of the building, but while that may well have been psychological, there is no explanation for what happened on the night of the Hartleys' farewell party. She was standing in the lounge area in front of the bar, talking to guests, when a glass tumbler from the back of the cabinet 'took off' and smashed at her feet. 'It must have flown in an arc to get to where I was standing,' she recalls. 'I remember making a joke of it and that Charlie – that's what I always called him – was upset at me leaving, but it was quite a weird experience.'

The only evidence of a 'presence' in the theatre proper was in 1972 when the actor/singer, Barry Hopkins, who was appearing in a week's variety, had the fright of his life. He was at a loose end one afternoon and decided to pop in to the White Rock to tidy up his dressing room. In those days the only entrance when the show was not on, was through the manager's office, from which he emerged at the back of the stalls. 'It was in total darkness,' Barry recalls. 'I was just getting my bearings when I was suddenly very conscious of *something* standing at my side. At the same time it became icy cold. The hair on my neck literally stood up and I just *knew* I was not alone.'

Barry panicked and stumbled through the auditorium to find someone backstage, and he ran into the arms of fellow performer, the impressionist Jenny Maynard, whose jaw dropped at the sight of his white face. 'When I appeared at the theatre in later years, I had my leg pulled about my ghost,' Barry admitted. 'It is possible I'm a little psychic and in normal circumstances I wouldn't have been frightened. But it happened so unexpectedly, I reacted without thinking.'

Sylvia Manser, who is currently in charge of the bars is convinced of paranormal activity from the number of times equipment has apparently functioned on its own; she also believes that the ghost is a woman, although she admits this is just a 'feeling' without any evidence. The most common occurrence is the mysterious turning off of the pumps' gas supply when there is no one about. Having inspected the circular taps, I did not need to be reminded that they need a firm twist of the wrist to turn them to the off position, so there is no possibility of them 'slipping' of their own accord.

When Sylvia opens up the bar, she also has to unlock the door to the cellar, where the beer and lemonade stocks are kept, after which nobody can get in without going past her (the other door from cellar to street is kept locked most of the time). 'If someone got in and turned the gas off between licensing hours, I wouldn't be able to pull much more than a half pint or so,' she explained. 'But I've started serving at 5.30 and at 8 decided it was time to change barrels, whereupon I've gone in to turn off the taps before switching cylinders – and found they were already in the off position!' The same thing has happened with the lemonade when all four 'switch' type taps have been moved to the off position. Her experience is borne out by colleagues and by her predecessor, Marion Hartley.

The 'ghost' must be preoccupied with the White Rock bars because another incident which has happened several times is the lights in the dress circle bar coming on by themselves at night. The daily routine is for the person in charge to turn off all the lights from switches housed in a concealed cupboard, which is then locked. The door to the bar itself is also then locked, and the person with the keys moves in total darkness (except for light from the sea front outside) through the lounge swing doors, which are also locked. It is not unusual (in Marion Hartley's day too) for the person leaving to have gone downstairs – and then be told that he or she has left the bar lights on! Other lights, individually operated by key, have also come on, but the bar area represents a spectacular display. There are no faults on the lighting circuit, and it would not be possible for a practical joker with a set of spare keys to unlock and subsequently re-lock three doors before making an escape, in the time it takes the person-in-charge to get back.

The Connaught Theatre, Worthing, closed in January 1986 to a depressingly uncertain future, but fortunately for the town (and a drama-impoverished South Coast) reopened nine months later, following a comprehensive £250,000 'face-lift'. However, the new staff knew nothing about the theatre's history, or its supernatural reputation. Even though I was able to recruit the assistance of local psychic investigator, Charles Walker, the results of our efforts were still to prove inconclusive. I can only hope that someone will turn up further evidence in the future.

Several theatre people had referred me to 'the ghost at Worthing', but the first recorded sighting was not until 1974 when there were reports of a grey lady seen in two of the dressing rooms. An account in the Worthing Gazette in July of that year credits a twenty-year-old Middlesex Polytechnic student, who had a 'walk-on' part in the current production, as seeing 'a grey lady with a white face and something on her head, vanishing into the wall'. The eye-witness, Angelica Clayton, supported by a girl friend, added that the figure was moving past a rail of clothes, but was actually above the rail. With her interest in history, she was able to date the costume to the Elizabethan period. However, when Charles

Walker heard of the incident and visited the theatre he found another witness who said that the ghost had been behind the rail, but because of the height of the rail would appear to have been walking on a different floor level. Charles had taken along a selection of costume designs from different periods, and his witness identified the clothing as Victorian. 'I suspect the student was influenced by being interested in a particular period,' he speculated.

In fact, we shall never know because thirteen years later neither of us has been able to locate her. Nor has it been possible to establish if there was any building on the site, or in the immediate vicinity of where the Picturedrome was built, which might have given some clue to the ghost's identity.

The second sighting was in August 1987 when fifteen-year-old Joseph Hall, spending his summer holidays at the theatre as a trainee, went underneath the stage to fetch something – and ran into the ghost on the spiral staircase. The young man panicked and did not stop to study her more closely, but was able to describe her as Victorian. Stage manager, Stephen Holroyd, accepts that Joseph saw what he claims. 'He shot up the stairs, white as a sheet. You always get a chilly feeling near the bottom of the spiral staircase. Now, no one wants to work at night alone.'

Another local newspaper also reported the sounds of a piano playing by itself in another part of the complex but the 'witness' remained remarkably elusive when I tried to confirm this, so I must remain sceptical on that score.

8

GUARDIAN ANGELS

It is a commonly held theory that the more powerful an actor's aura, the more likely is the theatre to cling on to his or her spirit – in which case outstanding theatres such as The Old Vic, which has produced dominant personalities such as Lilian Baylis, and actors of the calibre of Sybil Thorndike, Edith Evans, Olivier, Gielgud, Richardson and Redgrave would have a profusion of ghosts bumping into each other. Yet for all its fascinating history, there is no documented ghost at The Old Vic, despite hair-raising stories that in the early days (it was opened in May 1818 as the Royal Coburg Theatre) it was haunted by an actress agonising in the role of Lady Macbeth, dramatically wringing bloodstained hands.

Nevertheless, the following story told me by veteran actor, Alan Foss, demonstrates how difficult it is to investigate reports unless they are followed up immediately. At the end of World War I, Alan's father, George R. Foss was directing a *weekly* Shakespearian repertory season at the theatre. One of his protégées was a young actor called Eric Ross, who held promise of future stardom.

Eric had already won high praise for his performance as Hamlet, and was scheduled to play Brutus in a production of *Julius Caesar*. But the season coincided with a deadly epidemic of Spanish Flu, which struck down four members of the cast, of which *three* actually died – including Eric Ross, who was to be sorely missed. But, as we know, the show must go on, and replacements were found – despite the critical shortage of actors; many having been killed in the war, and many survivors still not having returned from the army.

On the opening night, during the orchard scene, several members of the audience were puzzled that one of the conspiritors remained apart from the others, almost as though he was not directly involved, but was eavesdropping

99

on the proceedings. Indeed, after the curtain, three people approached the director separately for an explanation, although no one would have been surprised to be told that a late replacement had not known his part properly. Yet to George Foss the scene had run as smoothly as the rest of the play, and he could not understand what they were talking about; he had seen the conspirators as a tight-knit little group.

But the more he enquired, the more confusing the response because most people – like him – had seen nothing unexpected, while a few had been aware of one actor who seemed to be 'out of step' with his fellow performers. His final check was with an acquaintance who had been in a box directly above the stage, whose reply was: '. . . the chap on his own? Oh, you mean Eric Ross?!' At least one person in that audience had no doubt that the young actor torn so tragically from the theatre he loved, had returned to ensure that everything went well on opening night!

Those who scoff at the idea of theatre ghosts should meet Edi [sic] Swan, technical director of the 1,800 seat His Majesty's Theatre, Aberdeen, built in 1906, but which did not claim a ghost until 1942 when a stagehand was accidentally killed. Cautious, Mr Swan is likely to respond tongue in cheek, dismissing out of hand some of the wilder stories, and possibly finding it easier to go along with others without argument. Yet, while his attitude is wholly rational, his own experience in the theatre leaves little doubt of the existence of a benevolent force, even if he is not sure of the form it takes.

'Jake', the generally accepted ghost, was already well established when Mr Swan joined the theatre. The accident had happened when a circus was performing, and a stage hoist was overloaded and over-ran the brake, killing John (Jake) Murray. Sightings and weird noises began to mount, eventually bestowing on the ghost (to use Mr Swan's description) a 'charisma far and above his original personality'. Inevitably, most of the creaks, groans and bangs were caused by natural means such as the hemp flying system with a wooden grid and fly floor and six miles of manilla hemp rope – a suspicion that was confirmed when the system was replaced with concrete and steel during major renovations in 1980–2, and such noises stopped overnight.

However, long before then it had become accepted practice to blame any unusual incident on 'Jake'; if something went missing and turned up later it would be blamed on Jake, rather than waste time conducting an investigation. In any case, not everything could be as easily dismissed as creaks and groans. Jake was actually seen more than once on the bridge to the fly floor; his footsteps, clearly identified as such, were heard, and when he 'walked' along what in this theatre they know as the Lambeth Walk, a long dark passage leading from the balcony to the fire escape stairs, the temperature would drop to freezing – with no rational cause. In fact, when the building was taken over by the contractors Taylor Woodrow in 1980–2, a night watchman was employed to keep an eye on valuable equipment. His guard dog was a large Alsatian called 'Savage' who behaved impeccably – until he was required to enter the Lambeth Walk, when he would sit back on his haunches and lay his ears back, while the fur on the back of his neck would bristle; a common reaction among guard dogs working in haunted buildings.

Edi Swan does not like putting tags on the theatre's ghost. 'I'm not even sure it is a single ghost as we understand the term. This place has been played by all the great artistes over the years – wonderful characters such as Wolfit,' he told me, 'and I wonder what happens to the enormous build-up of *energy*. But what I do believe is that some supernatural force keeps a protective eye on us.' His own experiences have been on two levels, some light-hearted, and others very much more serious.

When Mr Swan was the resident scenic artist he was in the habit of working into the night. Regularly, when painting, he would break off – putting his brush down by the sink, yet when he went to pick it up later, it was on the work table several feet away. 'I'm aware that scientists would say my tiredness was playing tricks – that I was disorientated into forgetting my last action and remembering a couple earlier. But I began to make a point of concentrating on what I was doing, so I know it wasn't happening by accident. Then I found the solution. At one time, in a fit of exasperation, I exclaimed: "Will you leave my brushes alone, Jake!" – and it stopped.'

It seems that Jake does not wait to be asked if he can be of assistance. During the 1958–59 season Edi was working late

101

as usual and fell down some stairs. The pain was so acute he was convinced he had broken an ankle (in fact, it was a bad sprain) and he needed medical attention urgently. The good news was that the hospital's Accident and Emergency unit was just at the back of the theatre; the bad was that access to it was not feasible. It would have entailed having to limp or crawl down the backstairs, from stage level to the basement, through the scenery dock and across Woolmanhill Street – the snag being that the door to the scenery dock was always locked at night, complete with chain and padlock. The job was the responsibility of the resident stage manager, Bert Ewen, who was very meticulous in everything he did. With sinking heart Edi contemplated the alternative route, but since that meant going down the same stairs, through the auditorium, and out by the foyer front of house before getting to the street – and *then* to somehow negotiate two more streets, he doubted whether he could make such a journey on hands and knees.

Conscious that he was wasting time, but desperate, Edi plumped for the direct route. Yet when he reached the scenery dock door, the padlock was there but not shut, and the chain loose. It was such a surprise that it took several seconds for him to accept his good fortune. Next day the stage manager vehemently denied he had failed to lock and padlock the door; it was something he did automatically. Edi Swan cannot be certain that the padlock was opened by some unearthly force, but he finds it even more difficult to accept that Bert Ewen, a man of machine-like efficiency, should so out of character, suddenly forget an integral part of his job – that night of all nights.

His belief in a guardian angel was strengthened by another late night incident. He was spraying gold paint on scenery when the nozzle jammed. Probably through tiredness, he stuck a pin into the hole to unclog the paint and it 'exploded' in his face, temporarily blinding him. 'I was in great pain and totally dazed,' he recalls, 'all I knew was that I had to get to the props room where there was a tap so I could wash out my eyes. But I'd lost all sense of direction. The safety curtain was up and I could have crawled downstage and fallen into the pit. But it was as though something took control of my actions – guiding me – and within seconds I was at the tap.'

There have also been reports of the ghost of a woman who used to walk across the foyer at His Majesty's, but it is assumed she is connected with premises that stood on the site before it was a theatre.

The more flamboyant a character, the more likely the assumption after death that he or she was the perpetrator of supernatural activity in the place most associated with them. Proof is another matter. Over the years there have been a number of rumours that the Duke of York's theatre in London's St Martin's Lane, is haunted by the ghost of Violet Melnotte, an eccentric and very quarrelsome actress who built the place in 1892, and retained varying degrees of control until her death in 1935.

In time rumour becomes folklore, attaining an element of authority that dismisses the need for proof, or even proper evidence. It is known, for example, that Miss Melnotte lived upstairs and would watch plays from a private box, so when strange noises were heard and the heavy door to her box would slam as though by someone in bad humour, it was inevitable that the reaction was a shrug at the action of a cantankerous old lady. However, while in hindsight we can recognise how wild many assumptions are, we cannot easily provide an explanation. I have seen the door to the box and the private room leading to it and know it would take the equivalent of a gale to shut it without human intervention.

Even more intriguing is an unexplained incident backstage in January 1980 which could be shrugged off as an individual's good luck, but could equally be attributed – if not to a ghost then to the intervention of a benevolent force. Shortly after being taken over by Capital Radio, the building underwent a face-lift with 'outside' decorators doing front of house, while theatre staff concentrated on backstage renovation because of the degree of technical skill required. In the usual race against time, Max Alfonso, the master carpenter, was in the habit of working very late to finish off what he might be doing at that time.

One night he was occupied with painting the stage walls and ceiling with black paint, for which it was necessary to use a 30ft high unit-assembled scaffold on wheels. In retrospect he realised it was not sensible to work alone at that height and in those conditions, but through a combination of tiredness and anxiety not to delay, Max was prepared to cut a few corners. Nor did he even apply the brakes on the tower's wheels, thinking that his weight and the full 10 litre can of paint would stabilise the platform.

Another fact he had overlooked in his haste was that, working in a corner, the steps to the adjoining props area prevented the tower from standing flush to the wall. At any other time he would have descended, and used an ordinary ladder for that section of the ceiling. Instead, he chose to stretch – leaning over as far as he could – and moments later the tower was tilting over towards the wall a few feet away. Simultaneously the tin of paint crashed down, continuing to alter the centre of gravity. As the top of the platform touched the wall, Max was doubly conscious of the wheels starting to move away. He froze, concentrating on how he might get down uninjured; the slightest movement causing the wheels to turn. Since remaining where he was meant crashing thirty feet to the stage within seconds, he would lose little by attempting to climb down, so gingerly he clambered on to the outside of the scaffolding – all the time feeling like a novice skater balancing precariously on roller skates that would not stand still. Fortunately, with his next move he was able to stretch out and grab a water pipe; half clambering, half jumping the rest of the way to the stage. It was while he was still catching his breath that the tower finally crashed down.

Years later the incident remains imprinted on his memory. 'The combination of brand new stage with its smooth hardboard surface, and the tower's new wheels, was like operating on a skating rink,' he told me. 'Once the wheels started to move there was nothing to stop them, and yet in mid-action *something* stopped them – long enough for me to get to safety. I've gone over the incident a thousand times in my mind and there is no "technical" explanation. All I know is that something saved me from serious injury. Funny, I've often had a feeling that someone was watching over what goes on in the theatre.'

9

SOUND OF MUSIC

The 'old' Palace Theatre, at Westcliff, now the nucleus of an attractive modern arts centre, claims a resident ghost known as 'George', although the real identity of what could well be a supernatural entity is open to question. Named the New Palace when built in 1912, the opening show was an intriguing combination of drama, variety and film. Yet the venture apparently ran into financial difficulties, as a result of which the proprietor hanged himself – giving rise to the first hint of a ghost, albeit one kindly disposed towards the place.

A year later the theatre became known as the Palace of Varieties, establishing a reputation as a somewhat grand music hall. Between the wars it was a touring theatre and then struggled for a number of years before being revitalised in 1970 when Southend County Borough council, which now owned the property, set up a Trust to establish a repertory company and raise the funds for extensive redecoration. Adopting a forward-looking policy, the Trust realised the need for a small 'intimate' studio theatre in which to stage small-scale presentations which would be dwarfed by the superb but traditional Edwardian auditorium. In 1980, land owned by the council adjoining the theatre became available, and within two years the new complex had been added.

There had been sporadic reports of a ghost, but it was not until the 1970s when the theatre was occupied on a round-the-clock basis, that they became more persistent. On one occasion in 1975 the company designer was working through the night, painting scenery. The building was empty and locked when, in the early hours she broke off to go to the toilet. On the stairs she came face to face with a woman in white. As she stared in disbelief the apparition disappeared. Hardly conclusive evidence, perhaps, since she was undoubtedly tired – a state in which her imagination might have played tricks –

but on the other hand she was preoccupied with the need to get her job finished and ghosts had not entered her mind; in any case, the only previous reports had been of 'George'.

Dave Bartlett, the current company stage manager, had a weird experience in 1977 when he was assistant to his predecessor. The theatre was closed and the two of them were occupied with various chores when they heard the piano on stage being played. The music was classical and the performance of professional standard, far beyond the prowess of anyone connected with the theatre – if there had been a musician around – but they knew the building to be empty.

Cautiously – taking courage in that there were two of them – they went to investigate, expecting to find a joker, splitting up to cover the only two approaches to the stage. The music continued until they were actually standing on the stage – when it suddenly stopped. There was nobody at the piano, yet there had been no time for anyone to get away – quite apart from the fact that both exits had been covered. Both men are convinced that it was the piano on stage they had heard, and not some pre-set tape recorder. Some*thing* had been playing it.

Two years later the resident stage manager was painting one of the dressing rooms alone on a Sunday morning, when he felt a firm hand on his shoulder. Unfortunately, he panicked and fled. There have also been a number of incidents difficult to categorise, such as 'complaints' from members of the public, unaware of the ghost stories, about the strange 'behaviour' of seats in the gallery (upper circle), maintaining that for no apparent reason there were sudden indentations, as might be made by someone sitting down in the unoccupied seat next to them – accompanied by the 'rustle' of leather being pressed down. 'I could swear someone was sitting down in the empty seat next to me,' was the general reaction. Imagination? Perhaps, but it has happened frequently.

Evidence perhaps of its elegant history, Eastbourne still manages to support *four* theatres in the summer season, of which two claim a resident ghost – the Devonshire Park, built in 1884, and the Royal Hippodrome, 1883. However, evidence in support of the former is inconclusive, while I have failed

completely to find anything to substantiate the legend associated with the latter.

The reported ghost at the Devonshire Park, spotted by a
number of people in recent years, is that of a violinist, dressed
for a performance, but nobody has been able to explain his
presence. One possibility offered by present manager, Roger
Neil (who came here from the Royal Hippodrome) is that the
theatre has a tradition of pantomime supported by an orchestra, and that the violinist might have been a 'regular' who
loved the building; but no musician has died on the premises
or is even known to have had any special relationship.

Nevertheless, a clearly defined figure – usually carrying a
violin and bow, and dressed in black 'tails', with white shirt
and bow-tie, is more intriguing than the grey or white 'mist'
in human form so often reported. Perhaps the most vivid
impression was received by former theatre electrician Geoff
Standfield when he was alone in the theatre on a Sunday
morning in 1968. Mr Standfield was setting the spots from
the balcony just above the orchestra pit, when he looked
down and saw the solitary figure of the violinist. The distance between them was short and his view unobstructed. It
was not a matter of a figure looking like a musician; it *was* a
musician. 'Then he gave a few bows and disappeared into thin
air,' Mr Standfield maintains. 'It was absolutely amazing.'
Having locked the theatre door behind him, and knowing no
one else was in the building, he rushed downstairs to double-
check but there was nothing to be seen. Another person who
had a clear view of the violinist was the company manager of
a touring production; a man who did not know the story of
a resident ghost.

The most recent sighting in 1987 was less clear. Steven
Gausden, who had not long taken over as doorman and who
was relatively new to the theatre, was locking up one evening
about thirty minutes after the performance ended. Knowing
the usherettes had cleared all levels he started with the upper
circle, and was crossing the seats towards an exit door when
his attention was captured by a dark figure moving between
the front stalls and the orchestra rail. His natural reaction was that someone had been missed by the usherettes, and
been locked in. By now everyone else, including the manager,

107

had gone. Intending to go down to 'rescue' the unfortunate patron, Steven called down, but the figure continued on its way. 'The house lights were not on so I couldn't make out a face,' Steven insists. 'In fact, my first impression was of a darkish shadow, but then I realised it was solid enough. When there isn't much light, you tend to pick out the small patches, or where it might be reflected. I distinctly remember the brass rail in front of the orchestra pit, and as the figure passed across, the light reflected was cut out. Whatever it was reached the end of the stalls and then disappeared, but it was dark enough in that corner to confuse me for a moment; all I know is that the exit door at that spot was locked and nothing could have got out, or in . . .'

Finding no trace of a customer, Steven finished his rounds, not giving the incident much thought until he reported to Roger Neil, next day. When the manager asked if what he had seen might have been the violinist, he was really confused. What violinist? He had never heard of the Devonshire Park ghost. Frustrating though they might be, the very vagueness of such reports, in my opinion, adds to their authenticity; fabricated stories tend to be very much more spectacular. Having met Steven Gausden, I believe he saw what he claims, and that his imagination was not playing tricks. It is a fact that the person charged with locking up a theatre at night gets on with the job, and does not have the time or inclination to daydream; furthermore, eyes get accustomed to the semi-darkness, and I would not doubt the ability of someone like Steven to see something that most people could only make out with the benefit of the house lights.

When it was built in 1884, the Devonshire Park Theatre, with its stuccoed exterior and twin flanking Italianate towers, was regarded as one of the most perfectly constructed playhouses outside London. Yet within twenty years, the brilliant Frank Matcham was brought in to carry out improvements in design as well as the facilities. Since then it has featured many of the outstanding entertainers of legitimate theatre and music hall. The Royal Hippodrome, opened a year earlier as the Theatre Royal (the name being changed around 1904) was better known as a palace of varieties, and its history is just as distinguished. The ghost legend of a long-term stage manager who fell to his death from the fly floor, is dramatic enough, befitting a grand Victorian theatre – but proving it is another matter. The death is not documented and although there are rumours of a ghostly figure with a flat cap, I have not been able to trace one former employee or artiste who has had a personal experience of anything, other than 'feelings' about the atmosphere.

Captivated as we are by the great names of theatre history it is easy to overlook the enormous contribution made to the nation's culture by largely forgotten men and women – such as J. W. Boughton, in Portsmouth. In 1900 he employed the services of Frank Matcham to rebuild the local Theatre Royal, and almost at once began planning the construction of a new playhouse in adjoining Southsea. When a rival consortium threatened to beat him to it, he secretly set Matcham to work on his own initiative and at his own expense, and 1907 saw the opening of the unusually attractive King's Theatre, which today is probably the only major playhouse still in private hands.

The Boughton theatre tradition has been maintained through four generations; appropriately, one of his actress great grand-daughters, Kate O'Mara, played in *The Exorcist* at Southsea in 1983. However, while Commander Reginald Cooper the administrator, and husband of the proprietor, Joan Cooper, believes in ghosts (having seen one at a factory he once owned), he is sceptical of stories that his beloved theatre is haunted; since the Coopers took over in 1960 there has not been one incident he regards as totally convincing. A few years ago the stage management team set up a tape recorder to switch on in the early hours. When the tape was played next day, initially all that could be heard were 'natural' sounds, such as the creaking of wood – yet one which could not be explained was the intermittent sound of a single piano note. However, neither Commander Cooper or the resident stage manager believe in a supernatural cause. 'We simply don't know,' they admit, 'but a technical explanation is still the more likely bet.'

Sightings without substantiated evidence are regarded as 'not proven' – events which simply have no explanation. I spoke to Mark Skipper, the electrician, who has had two experiences which come into this category. One was when the theatre was empty and Mark was walking in a passage at dress circle level. Passing the open door of a box, he saw a man sitting in the facing box. He could see across the auditorium quite clearly and since there should not have been anyone there he retraced his steps to take a more careful look. The man, dressed in brown, was no one he recognised, and as he stared the figure just vanished. Could it have been Mr Boughton? As no one else has ever seen the same figure, we may never know.

NOT NECESSARILY GHOSTS

If we should ever encounter an apparition, the chances are that it will be in earthly form, although we know that flesh and bones have no relevance after death. So is it possible for the human spirit to adopt another form? Highly improbable, surely, if we believe that a ghost is an image of the human body locked in time. However, the answer could be different if we put aside preconceived ideas on the subject.

At the start of every pantomime season, at the Theatre Royal, Bath, staff and performers wait for the appearance of a peacock butterfly; they know it will bring good fortune. The superstition is associated with the Maddox family who ran the theatre between 1926–76. Like most long-term managers they left their mark on the theatre, but are perhaps best remembered for the revival of the family pantomime, a tradition that is still maintained and attracts the country's top performers. In 1938, for the production of *Aladdin*, Reg Maddox, head of the family, decided to create a butterfly ballet, with the dancers dressed accordingly. The backdrop was to be a huge peacock butterfly (particularly colourful but named because of the large eye-spots on all four wings resembling the eyes on a peacock's tail feathers). At the lighting rehearsal a dead butterfly fell among the actors and technicians. At any other time it would have gone unnoticed because although the peacock butterfly has a life expectancy of ten months – much longer than other British varieties – it is usually in hibernation in December. It might have been more than coincidence, because shortly afterwards Reg Maddox had a heart attack and died the same night.

Fearing it was a bad omen management decided to take out the butterfly sequence. In the following year the Maddox family intended to produce the same pantomime minus the butterfly ballet, but Reg's son, Frank, was directing on stage when a peacock butterfly appeared – in the same place and at the same time. He was so excited by the coincidence that he decided on the spot to restore the ballet. It met with great success.

When the theatre was renovated, one of the few old props that was kept and still hangs at the back of the fly tower, is the original 12ft x 8ft butterfly backdrop. Retained as a good-luck charm, there is nevertheless an instinctive fear that if a live butterfly does not appear before the start of the pantomime – particularly in the case of *Aladdin*, the spell might be broken. This is why Leslie Crowther, playing 'Wishy Washy' in *Aladdin*, making his entrance in the opening performance – the matinee of Boxing Day, 1979 – was just the slightest bit uneasy. The butterfly had not yet appeared.

However, there was nothing in his manner to indicate anything was on his mind as he marched on and set about establishing a rapport with the audience. Leslie Crowther is a 'natural' performer, but when he got a ripple of amusement in an unexpected place he glanced up, and – framed in the spotlight was a peacock butterfly descending majestically, as though relishing its moment of glory, until it came to rest on the right lapel of his jacket. He waited and it flew down to hover around his flies – to the even greater amusement of the audience – before returning to his lapel. Then, conscious of a show to do, he cupped it in his hands and released it in the wings, returning to tell the audience he would explain the significance at the end. The same butterfly remained in the theatre for several weeks. Bearing in mind butterflies should not be around at this time of year, it is interesting to note that in another year Honor Blackman, dressed as the wicked fairy for *Jack and the Beanstalk*, also attracted a butterfly as she stood in the wings.

But theatre superstition being what it is, it is worth adding that a *dead* butterfly would be regarded as a bad omen. Some years ago at Bath a company manager looking for one of his actors, found a dead butterfly in his dressing room. The same night the missing actor was found at his lodgings. He had hanged himself!

Anthony Bate is not only an outstanding actor, he is one of the more intelligent; someone who thinks about the characters he plays and tries to understand their behaviour. One of his more challenging roles – heightened, perhaps, by the physical dissimilarities – was that of Stalin in *Masterclass*, David Pownall's savage satire on the Soviet attitude towards freedom of expression in the arts.

The play was on tour in 1984, arriving at Swansea's Grand Theatre for a week in October. The cast were unaware of the resident ghost, and in any case Anthony Bate is, by his own admission, a 'profound sceptic'. His attitude then, he told me, was that such things always happen to other people, and while not blinkered to the possibility of their existence, he would have welcomed some proper evidence. What happened to him at the Grand cannot be categorised as a ghost story, but a sequence of paranormal incidents that defy explanation. Remember, the play had been running successfully for a couple of months, the cast were thoroughly into their characters and word perfect, and there had been no problems at any stage. Similarly, the technical dress rehearsal in this theatre had gone without a hitch.

The play deals with the awesome intimidation of artistes – in this case musicians – by the political bureaucrats who were imposing their 'standards' on a whole spectrum of creative talent; having to toe the party line in the political sense may be objectionable (if understandable), but conforming to arbitrary standards set by people with no artistic qualifications is much worse. In one scene, Stalin is lecturing two of the great modern Russian composers, Prokofiev and Shostakovich, on their shortcomings. Critical of everything they have written, Stalin (behind his back labelled 'Tone Deaf Geoff from Georgia'), proceeds to demonstrate how to compose his idea of better music. With one finger he picks out a banal tune to the words, 'My lone-ly heart is a car-a-van.'

Anthony Bate knew the simple tune by heart, yet on the first night the eighth and ninth notes (the same E above middle C) did not register, apart from the click of an unconnected key. Although disconcerted, he did not have time to dwell on the mishap, hoping that his performance was in other respects good, and that the audience were appreciating the play. Fortunately, most of the audience did not react to the missing notes, assuming that this was merely another indication of the Soviet dictator's musical ignorance. However, the same thing happened on the second night, and convinced now that everyone would assume he had not played the piece correctly, he mentioned it to the stage manager – whose reaction, while sympathetic, was that the piano had been professionally tuned in preparation for the play.

To satisfy him, the piano was tuned again, and indeed when Anthony Bate – out of costume and make-up, ie as himself – tested the note it played normally. Yet during the matinee performance it happened again. 'By now, the story of the ghost was circulating,' he told me. 'On stage, four sets of eyes – quite apart from the whole stage management team – were riveted on that one key, and when it still didn't play, it was like a bombshell.'

The 'hoodoo' persisted in Wednesday evening's performance, and that night he lay in bed, worried and confused, praying that by the law of averages it could not happen again. 'Everyone had tried the note, and at no time did it misbehave – except when the pianist was Stalin,' he recalls. 'As it happens, the three actors on stage with me were all accomplished musicians, and they had instinctively been keeping one eye on the way my finger hit the keys. Furthermore, *immediately* after the incident, Frank Lazarus as Prokofiev had to sit down and improvise a tune, hitting the faulty note – which then played normally.'

The rebellious note continued to defy 'Stalin' on Thursday, Friday and Saturday – until the eighth and final performance on Saturday night when it seemed to relent, and play normally! There are those who like to believe that the mischief was caused by the theatre ghost who misinterpreted the atmosphere of 'evil' on stage as being real, and set out to spike the apparent villain's guns. That, surely, is stretching credibility. On the other hand, what is the explanation?

What more appropriate setting for a ghost than a musical play about the murderer Crippen? But while Michael Branwell's startling experience involving a disembodied face during a performance of *Crippen* at the Century Theatre, Keswick, in 1984, is not attributed to the supernatural, no one can offer a rational explanation.

Michael, then company and stage manager at the theatre,

which does not claim a resident ghost (although the administrator, Anthony Stott, has had a strange experience at another 'haunted' theatre), and his team – a DSM and two ASMs – were accustomed to working the lighting box, especially as it afforded the best overall view of what was going on. *Crippen* was a particularly hectic show for members of the stage management, and with 118 lighting cues alone, at least two of the team were in the box for most of the show.

In one scene, Genevieve Walsh, playing Belle Elmore, had a song which gave them a brief respite because there were no special lighting effects involved, not even a follow spot. But as Michael, relaxing for a moment, watched from the box, he was disconcerted by what looked like reflected pink and white lights in the shape of a face, moving around the stage as though taking an interest in the performance. What an unusual trick of the light, he thought! Yet no matter how much he tried to change his perspective, the 'face' remained – only to disappear at the end of the song.

At the end of the show, when they were comparing notes on the smooth running of the production, he mentioned the bizarre trick of the lights to his ASM, imagining it could only have been seen from where he had been standing, but not only had she seen the reflections, but also the face. The strange feature of the story is that the lights for the scene were no different from any other scene in the show – or, from any other play in all the time he was at The Century; the system was too 'primitive' to try anything more elaborate. Yet the reflections, if that is what caused the effect, had never happened before – and never again, apart from that one scene repeated several times during the run.

'Three hardbitten stage management people saw the face, separately and together, on several occasions,' Michael Branwell told me. 'Obviously I'm not claiming it as a ghost, but we considered every technical possibility, and four years later I'm still trying to puzzle it out!'

A small proportion of theatregoers who enjoy a play or musical might go again, but occasionally the relationship develops into a love affair when the fan finds it difficult to stay away. This is something that managers come to expect with a successful production, getting to know the regular visitors. Richard Schulman, for example, who retired in the early 1980s, recalls two nurses who each saw *The Canterbury Tales* fifty times (something he could understand, since he had seen Noel Coward's *Bitter Sweet* at least twenty times). That show had been running neck and neck with *Hair*, which had opened at the Shaftesbury Theatre from September 1968, and by coincidence he was to move to that theatre as manager. Built in 1911, the Shaftesbury stage has been a showcase for some of the great names, such as Sarah Bernhardt, and it seems appropriate that it should have been the home for five years of such an innovative 'tribal love-rock' production, *Hair*, which did much to change the face of the modern musical.

Mr Schulman's move to the Shaftesbury in 1973 coincided with its reopening after repairs to the roof which had collapsed, and he was soon acquainted with the story of a customer well known to the theatre staff, whose reappearance was awaited with bated breath. The reason for their anxiety was that the man, a regular theatregoer, had been fascinated by *Hair* from the outset. He liked a certain seat in the front of the stalls, and over the years was in the theatre so often that he became a friend. Towards the end of the run when it was no longer an automatic sell-out, the seat was kept permanently reserved, on the offchance that he would turn up.

One night he suggested the 'reservation' could lapse for a short spell as he was going into hospital the next day for an operation, but that he would be back to see the end of the run. About four days before *Hair* was due to close, in the middle of the night, the night watchman heard an alarming noise from the auditorium and discovered that a large section of the ceiling had fallen in. The debris, a mixture of large chunks of masonry and powdery dust was widespread, but had not caused much other damage, although a large piece had scored a direct hit on one seat in the front stalls, demolishing it. It was, of course, the seat reserved for their regular customer. Members of the staff took that as an omen, suspecting the incident had coincided with his death in hospital. Unfortunately, no one knew his address so they were unable to check, but one thing is certain – he never visited the theatre again.

In the mid-1970s, a series of storms and high winds damaged the lantern (a safety device which, in the event of a fire on stage, while the sprinkler system is activated, creates a chimney effect, sucking smoke through the roof) below the roof of the Leicester Haymarket theatre. The winds took out panes of glass in the ventilator windows, and it was the job of then head carpenter, Colin Watson, to replace the glass with plywood. Annoyingly, another gale on the next night took out the plywood too. However, when the winds had died down next morning, just after 7 am, he again started up the ladder for the roof.

As Mr Watson approached the grid, seventy feet off the stage, his eyes came level with a pair of women's brown court shoes, then brown lisle stockings and finally a full view of a smartly clothed young woman standing on the grid. She was dressed for outdoors, complete with hat and gloves. Startled, although the significance of her presence had not really registered, he greeted her politely and continued climbing the final eight or so feet to the lantern.

Anyone who has stood next to a ladder leading to the grid in any large theatre will appreciate that climbing vertically is a daunting task for most people, and Mr Watson's surprise was only tempered by the fact that many people pass through a theatre – actors and visiting stage management personnel who might not immediately be recognisable to him. But it was not until he had climbed into the lantern that he did a 'double take' – what was a strange young woman doing up there at that time in the morning! He climbed out and descended to the grid, intent on asking who she was – but in that second or two, she had vanished. If she had gone down the ladder he would have caught her up; the only other possible exit was a catwalk crossing the top of the auditorium, but there was no sign of her.

Colin Watson, now technical co-ordinator, explained: 'The only people in the theatre apart from me were the cleaners, but no one had seen her. The front of house was locked, and the only way in or out was the stage door and there were cleaners in that area throughout. I'm not saying she was a ghost – she certainly looked real enough to me – but her presence on the grid, or

117

even how she got in and out of the building, was inexplicable.'

The Royal Opera House in London's Covent Garden, built in 1858, has a fascinating history – yet no ghost to anyone's knowledge; but that isn't to say there haven't been some strange incidents over the years. John Jordan, now stage manager of the Grand Opera House, Belfast, was employed there as an electrician in 1974, and on one occasion needed to work through the night on a production of *Don Giovanni*. At 3am he had to go to the grid to do some rigging. Covent Garden was one of the few theatres which had the 'luxury' of a lift for this purpose, and to get to the dome and the armoury workshop just below.

John used it to go up to what is known as the iron roof, where it was pitch black, and where he had to use a torch. On finishing, he found his way back to summon the lift, but when he was within ten feet of it, he heard the contacts operate and the motor start humming. By the time he reached the closed gate the lift was on its way up. Since he had not pressed the button, he assumed that it was being 'driven' by his assistant, coming to help him, albeit a little late – but when the lift cage arrived, it was empty. On his descent he was left to puzzle out how a manually operated lift could work without anyone pressing the button.

The Alexandra Theatre in Birmingham claims a resident ghost, but even those who believe in its existence do not attribute every unexplained incident to the supernatural. In 1986, a new computerised lighting board was installed. With the old board taken out and all power to the stage disconnected (with every individual light immobilised) the whole area was in darkness – apart from a solitary white spot over the centre stage. The electricians stared, mystified that a light could operate without electricity – but assuming as each second ticked away that it would soon go out.

However, twenty minutes later, the spot was still on! Chief electrician, Alan Galloway told me: 'Between the old board and individual lights there were control stages and no way that power could have gone past the first – let alone all three. We explored every possibility, but eventually had to give up; we removed the offending light and connected up the new system, after which everything behaved normally. We still have no explanation.'

On the subject of technical problems, at Oxford's Apollo touring theatre in the mid-1970s, when it was known as the New Theatre, electrician Adrian Redmond was working in his office long after the show, having seen everybody out and locked up. However, he had forgotten to turn off the tannoy and was suddenly aware of voices from the stage coming through the speaker in his office. There were apparently a number of people, and he described them as 'chatting away like mad'. Mystified, he hurried down to the stage but found it in darkness (as he had left it earlier). There was no one in sight. But returning to his office, he was unnerved to hear the voices again, and decided to call it a night! I have heard of tannoy equipment picking up radio programmes, but Adrian insists the voices were definitely coming from the stage.

Although Shakespeare stands head and shoulders above other British playwrights, it is perhaps indicative of the British character that he remains the *only* writer to be honoured with two major playhouses dedicated to his work. In the case of a great modern playwright – George Bernard Shaw – the only theatre in the world devoted solely to him, is the Shaw Festival playhouse at Niagara Falls. The nearest we seem to have come in the United Kingdom was the Shaw season at the Malvern Festival, introduced by Sir Barry Jackson in 1929, which played for a number of years but eventually ran out of steam. In fact, some of Shaw's plays had their British premiere at Malvern, and the Irishman forged close ties with Malvern in the 1930s, so it was not surprising that after his death in 1950 a rumour sprang up that his ghost had returned to the theatre. Remembering GBS's strong views on the supernatural, nothing could be more unlikely; or, as the great man might have retorted: 'over my dead body!'.

Indeed, the theatre's management remains sceptical of *any* ghost, and while I am not in a position to dispute that conviction, there have undoubtedly been some strange stories about the building, opened in 1885. The writer and director, Michael Bakewell, worked at the Festival Theatre for a couple of months in 1966 when Bernard Hepton, better known as an actor, directed a summer season dedicated to

Shaw. Michael's involvement was to co-direct a revival of the eighteenth-century French comedy, *The Confidence Tricks.*

Despite the fact that early in rehearsals he and others heard the distinct sound of footsteps in the flies – when they knew there was nobody there – Michael was not impressed with the gossip he had heard about Shaw's ghost. Nor was he put out when at the lighting rehearsal a number of seats in the dress circle took it upon themselves to tip up and down at random. He was too engrossed in his directing responsibilities to pay much attention. However, after the dress rehearsal, by which time everyone was exhausted, he and the cast adjourned to the pub. Too late, he realised he had left his notes for the actors where he had been sitting in the dress circle – which meant going back. Having borrowed the theatre keys, he found the building in darkness. Not knowing where the light switches were, he managed to grope his way to the dress circle. Even to those not unduly sensitive, darkness can be disorientating but when he got to the circle it was no great problem 'feeling' his way down to the front row. He remembers being very conscious of the oppressive silence, so that when one of the seats tipped up it made him jump.

'Although it scared me momentarily, I was rational enough to realise it was something that could happen, and had before,' he told me. 'Then it happened again somewhere else – and again. By now, I had found my seat and the notes, so it was not a question of staying the night and having to put up with these intermittent noises. In any case, I was subconsciously reassuring myself that what was happening was quite natural, that it was something to do with the temperature in the auditorium. But I knew it wasn't that, because the sounds were too deliberate . . . a heavy *plonk*, then plonk, plonk, plonk. As I listened the momentum gathered pace, becoming frantic. The experience was a different dimension to anything I had ever encountered, and I was absolutely terrified. I stumbled out of the circle, feeling that *something* was there.'

It is one thing for a row of seats to tip in sequence, but there is no mechanical explanation for what happened to Michael Bakewell, when seats were going up and down individually, and at apparent random. He did not imagine it; it happened. Yet equally surprising there were no further incidents of any kind, although, admittedly, no one paid a visit to the auditorium after dark – not on their own.

It was the theatre historian and writer, John Kennedy Melling who passed to me a few of the more interesting experiences of his friend, Danny Ross, speculating as he did as to whether the actor had possessed certain psychic powers. 'Danny was a tough, down to earth North Countryman,' he recalls, 'yet he must have been very sensitive to have picked up the manifestations he did.' One incident occurred during a production of *Dracula* at the old Theatre Royal, Oldham. When the play was running, he arrived at the theatre one day to find the leading actor, Wally Thomas, not only ahead of him, but already in costume and full make-up – despite the fact that as the star, his first appearance on stage was not until well into the first act.

However, strange though it seemed, it was not his business so he made no comment, proceeding to his dressing room where he began to prepare for his own entrance. He had hardly started when he was interrupted by the arrival of Wally Thomas still in his street clothes – which meant that the person he had just recognised as the actor he knew so well, had *not* been! (It would have been impossible for any actor to have cleaned off his make-up properly and changed back into his own clothes in the few minutes that had elapsed, even if he had been eccentric enough to have wanted to do so.)

So who or what had Danny Ross seen moments earlier? He had not been drinking; nor did he imagine the incident. If one believes in the *time* element as an explanation of the spectral image, one might speculate on the ghost of a living person. Or could it have been precognition, or extra-sensory perception? This seems a reasonable possibility because a few years earlier Ross had been touring Germany with a show for British servicemen. Arriving under his own steam at his next destination, a theatre in the Rhine area, he introduced himself to his German hosts and asked to be shown to dressing room 15, where he found his name on the door. It was not until then that he realised he had never been to the theatre before, yet had known instinctively which dressing room he would be using!

In the nicest sense, there is undoubtedly something strange

121

at the Theatre Royal, Lincoln, but proving it is another matter. The longest serving member of the staff, Art Walker, the stage manager, has had no personal experience of the supernatural, but believes that certain incidents involving colleagues at different times defy rational explanation. I contacted the theatre after hearing rumours about seats in the auditorium behaving 'strangely', and in view of Mr Walker's understandably sceptical attitude, I posed the question somewhat diffidently. But he took me seriously.

'I've not been around when most of these things are supposed to have happened,' he conceded, 'but I had to be impressed by something that happened to Nigel Clarke, our electrician when we were in repertory. Nigel was not the sort of person to imagine things, but on one occasion he was scared out of his wits by what he described as a "terrible noise" coming from the seats – which so alarmed him he ran out of the theatre. He couldn't describe the type of sound except that it was not natural.' To complicate the issue, Mr Clarke now works overseas and I have been unable to get him to elaborate on his original account, but Mr Walker added that recently his own electrician also left in a hurry one night; his only explanation later being that 'something' had alarmed him and that he did not want to talk about it.

'I have to admit there have been a number of weird happenings over the years,' Mr Walker declares. 'During one amateur production, we put an actress in the top dressing room – but before long she came running down in hysterics, saying she had seen something – but she was too frightened to say any more. I'm afraid we were too busy getting the show on to pay much attention to her. On another occasion, someone new in the box office asked me if we had a ghost. She said she felt a "presence" in part of the dress circle where it seemed particularly cold. She arranged for one of her friends, who was a psychic to come in, and that person said there was definitely *something* supernatural in the circle. Unfortunately, what it is, or what happens to the seats, no one knows.'

Another attractive late Victorian building by Frank Matcham, the Cheltenham Everyman (known as the Opera House until 1960) has an unseen ghost which is supposed to be the spirit of a labourer who fell off some scaffolding during redecorations in 1927. Rumour has it that the spirit occupied a seat in the back row of the stalls, but there is no evidence of this – despite the fact that a clergyman watching a performance of *Tom Jones* in 1965 collapsed and died in that seat. However, those who believe in that ghost maintain that it was a benevolent spirit until a prediction by the clairvoyant Al Koran came true. Koran, who appeared in the early 1950s with a touring show told theatre staff that there would be serious financial problems which would result in the closure of the Opera House, and although the theatre would reopen, the upheaval would disturb the ghost.

In fact, as far as I have been able to ascertain, the resident ghost has never been seen, although there is good reason to suggest something was disturbed by the eighteen-month upheaval. For a time strange things would happen, such as fire hydrants coming on in the night by themselves. A number of backstage staff had weird experiences and Chris Heron, a company stage manager some ten years after the reopening, remembers incidents which happened to members of his team, including a flyman who, after one experience refused to go up alone. Although he could not explain what had alarmed him, he insisted that *something* had been up there. Throughout the book I have avoided references to 'feelings', since they do not constitute evidence, but there were incidents in the 1970s which affected groups of people, such as one late-night tea-break. Chris Heron recalls: 'There were five of us in the crew-room. Suddenly, I had a strong sense that we were waiting for someone else to arrive. Then I noticed the designer glancing towards the door, and when I asked why, he said he had the same feeling – indeed, we all did. It was a remarkable experience.'

However, something really frightening happened to Ernest Dyson who had joined the original company as a stagehand and had been asked to return to handle night security while the theatre was being prepared for reopening. One night in June 1959 the theatre was locked when he was joined by a couple of policemen for a cup of tea. Just after midnight they heard footsteps on the fly floor. Ernest, used to the normal theatre noises, was convinced that these were actually footsteps. Deciding to investigate, they split up – one policeman approaching from one ladder, and the second at the other side – but they found no one. The incident so unnerved the policemen that they decided they had other pressing duties back on the beat. Their hurried departure prompted Ernest to lock himself in one of the dressing rooms at stage level, after which other unusual noises convinced him of the wisdom of staying where he was for the night!

When he emerged in the morning, there in the centre of the stage were two 18ft scenery flats standing, *one on top of the other* – without any means of support. In a production, scenery is securely bolted and supported by counter-weights. A flat, no more than eighteen inches thick, would be very vulnerable without support; two would be impossible to balance – yet there in front of him was a structure 36ft high! 'Apart from the sheer impossibility,' Ernest assured me, 'it would have taken a small army to manhandle heavy flats on top of each other.' In fact, as soon as he moved nearer they crashed to the stage.

The 'versatility' of the Theatre Royal, St Helens – over the years offering the whole spectrum of entertainment from music hall to opera – makes it one of the most fascinating theatres in the North. The town's fourth Theatre Royal (second on the present site in Corporation Street), was designed by the brilliant Frank Matcham, opened in 1901, and is today one of only two industrially owned playhouses in the United Kingdom.

Despite its early successes – it was a 'home from home' for most North Country artistes, including Gracie Fields who 'tried out' a number of her famous songs (such as 'Walter') here – the general recession in show business in the 1950s culminated in its demise. Closed, it was in danger of becoming a derelict landmark of nostalgia when Pilkington, the glass manufacturers, bought the theatre in 1960. Refurbished and redesigned – reducing the seating capacity by a half to a mere 700 seats – the new playhouse made audience comfort one of its major features.

Like most 'live' theatres, the Royal has a vibrant atmosphere and is full of happy memories. Yet it is inevitable that a number of dramatic events on site, even before its opening at the start of the century (the previous much-loved theatre was destroyed by fire in the early hours of an October Friday the 13th) have resulted in a legacy of at least one visible ghost. In fact, even incidents which probably have no bearing on the supernatural seem, in other ways, to have links with what is – for want of a better heading – Fate. I've already mentioned Friday the 13th, so for those interested in the significance of numbers, how is this for a coincidence?

In the heyday of its reputation as a house of varieties, the Royal had an adagio act called Balliol and Merton. The team were rehearsing on a Monday when Carl, the male member of the act was injured in a fall and was carried to number one dressing room, where he died. Slim Ingram, the former manager, was interested enough in the theatre's history to investigate the incident, and he discovered that death occurred on the artiste's forty-seventh birthday – *and* that he had been born in the number one dressing room of what was then the Hippodrome (formerly Palace Theatre), only a couple of streets away.

Another typically strange story concerns an airman in World War II who begged accommodation for the night, and was allowed to sleep on a settee in the foyer. In the morning he was given a cup of tea by the cleaners and went on his way. Within the hour he had been arrested. A charge of murder was followed by conviction, and the man's eventual execution by hanging.

It may have been this somewhat loose connection with hanging that prompted Slim Ingram to jump to the conclusion that a former manager who committed suicide in his office in 1923, had hanged himself. The method is not important at this point, but several sightings of a ghostly figure in the dress circle are presumed to have been of that manager. The 'man in black' has been spotted on a number of occasions by actors from the stage, and by Mr Ingram who also realised that before the 1960s redesign, the manager's office had been situated at that spot.

The 'man in black' was seen in close-up for the first time in December 1986 by an usherette, Bernadette Critchley, during a performance of the play *Wait Until Dark*, about a terrorised blind woman who uses the darkness to turn the tables on a murderer. Bernadette was descending a staircase from the

125

auditorium into the stalls and half turned to realise that she was being followed by a man in black pinstripe trousers, a long black coat and black shoes with spats. She waited – no more than a second or two – until she had reached the bottom before turning to ask if she could help – but by then he had vanished.

By sheer coincidence – and unknown to her – the story of the ghost theory had appeared in a local newspaper forty-eight hours before, and the following morning Mr Ingram received a phone call from a woman who told him that the report had been sparse and inaccurate. She knew because her mother had discovered the body of the manager who killed himself. Death had not been from hanging, she pointed out, but gas poisoning; furthermore, when her mother found the body it was lying on the floor, covered with a long black overcoat. He had been wearing black pinstripe trousers, and shoes with spats. None of this had been known before.

INDEX